Vegetarian For Life

Over 150 Delicious Vegan-Vegetarian Dishes
Darlene Blaney, R.H.N., R.N.C.P.
Nutritional Consultant

First Edition - 1998
Second Edition - 1999

Design and Layout: Darlene and Ron Blaney

Photography: Blaine Andrusek

Food Styling: Darlene Blaney, Blaine Andrusek

email: blaneyd@cadvision.com

http://members.home.net/vegetarianforlife

Sundog Printing Limited, Calgary, AB, Canada

Table of Contents

Acknowledgments

It is important to acknowledge and thank the following people who contributed in some way to make this book a success:

Ron, my dear husband who encouraged and supported me in helping to make the publishing of this cookbook dream come true and spent endless hours typesetting.

Nathan and Reuben, my two sons who willingly sampled my creations and graded each dish as "Child Approved".

My mom Jennie Straub, who inspired and taught me to enjoy cooking at a young age.

My dad Daniel Straub, who ate even my "mess-ups" and still pretended to enjoy them.

Carolyn my sister and her husband Dave Good, who encouraged me to use my spiritual gifts and to do all that I am able.

Diana Straub-Clarke, my sister, for taking the time to proofread and test various recipes.

Laura Lepard, a close friend, who spent many hours in support in preparations for the photo shootings; and her husband Dale who inspired me with compliments and taste tested many of the recipes.

Customers, cooking school students, friends and family who suggested I put together a cookbook, helped name some of the recipes, then encouraged me to complete it.

Valerie and Ted Fitch, who helped me with valuable information, and created the unique, powerful title "VEGETARIAN FOR LIFE".

Blaine Andrusek, who spent quality time, creating quality, pictures! Special thanks for taking this project personally-the encouragement, support, and the friendship that developed.

Cathy and Jim Robertson who supported and helped me put the "finishing touches" on.

Sundog Printers who Printed and supported in the makings of this book.

Gary Acton from Sundog printers - a special Thank you for your patience, encouragement and support.

Last, but not least, my Best Friend Jesus Christ, who made me who I am today. May I continue to do all things to the Glory and Honor of God!

Thank you, may God bless each and every one of you!

Darlene Blaney

Introduction

My vegetarian experience began when I met my husband Ron 10 years ago. I was raised on meat and dairy products with a mixture of some vegetarian dishes and meat analogs (imitation meat products made of soy). I enjoyed helping out with various cooking schools from about age 10 onwards. Even then, the food I helped teach, did not inspire me to change my own diet. My husband was raised lacto-vegetarian, so I agreed to going off the meat would be okay as long as I was able to enjoy my cheese, milk and eggs. It was then I began to realize the difference of a vegetarian lifestyle. Occasionally I would crave some chicken and would weaken to have a piece. Each time I would become very sick for about 24 hours. I could not believe how heavy the meat was on my stomach and how it interferes with the digestion process. It was then that I made up my mind I was going to change for me, and began to research along with my husband further into the health of dairy products. At this time I was pregnant and not only did my health matter, but I was responsible for another life as well. Again the knowledge obtained from the research we gathered led us to omit eggs and all dairy products. I never imagined the day I would make this lifestyle change! The recipe search was on! I learned to supplement some of the ingredients in my previous recipes. They were able to remain family favorites, only healthier. At this point I wanted to teach others what I had learned and began to teach cooking classes in my home.

The excitement of watching people change their lifestyle, lose weight and correct various health problems inspired my husband and I to dedicate our lives to God and His health message. Together we opened a store "NATURE'S PROMISE HEALTH FOODS". A kitchen was built in the store to hold cooking schools. At this point our second child was born and we are proud to be raising both children as vegan-vegetarians.

We then opened a lunch counter and accepted many catering requests. With the countless requests for recipes, we improvised and created our own cookbook workbook, implementing it into our cooking class. This is when the dream of writing my own cookbook came about.

The joy and excitement of working with people led me to obtain my degree as a Registered Nutritional Consultant. As my time becomes more limited, I hope this cookbook will reach those I personally cannot have contact with and it will change their lives in the way these recipes changed my family's and my life. May you experience the same joy as you delight in the great taste and smell of cooking nutritionally!

CHOOSE HEALTH

WHOLE GRAINS
5 OR MORE SERVINGS A DAY

VEGETABLES
3 OR MORE SERVINGS A DAY

Vegetables are packed with nutrients; they provide vitamin C, beta-carotene, riboflavin, iron, calcium, fiber, and other vitamins. Dark green, leafy vegetables such as broccoli, collards, kale, mustard and turnip greens, chicory, or bok choy are especially good sources of these important nutrients. Dark yellow and orange vegetables such as carrots, winter squash, sweet potatoes and pumpkin provide extra beta-carotene. Include generous portions of a variety of vegetables in your diet. Serving size: 1 cup raw vegetables • 1/2 cup cooked vegetables

PHOTOS / LISA MASSON

THE NEW FOUR FOOD GROUPS

This group includes bread, rice, pasta, hot or cold cereal, corn, millet, barley, bulgur, buckwheat groats, and tortillas. Build each of your meals around a hearty grain dish—grains are rich in fiber and other complex carbohydrates, as well as protein, B vitamins and zinc. Serving size: 1/2 cup hot cereal • 1 ounce dry cereal • 1 slice bread

LEGUMES
2 OR MORE SERVINGS A DAY

Legumes—which is another name for beans, peas, and lentils—are all good sources of fiber, protein, iron, calcium, zinc, and B vitamins. This group also includes chickpeas, baked and refried beans, soy milk, tempeh, and texturized vegetable protein. Serving size: 1/2 cup cooked beans • 4 ounces tofu or tempeh • 8 ounces soy milk

FRUIT
3 OR MORE SERVINGS A DAY

Fruits are rich in fiber, vitamin C, and beta-carotene. Be sure to include at least one serving each day of fruits that are high in vitamin C—citrus fruits, melons, and strawberries are all good choices. Choose whole fruit over fruit juices, which do not contain very much fiber. Serving size: 1 medium piece of fruit • 1/2 cup cooked fruit • 1/2 cup juice

PRINTED ON RECYCLED PAPER

Be sure to include a good source of vitamin B-12, such as fortified cereals or vitamin supplements.

PHYSICIANS COMMITTEE FOR RESPONSIBLE MEDICINE • P.O. BOX 6322 • WASHINGTON, DC 20015 • (202) 686-2210

"Speciality Items" Glossary

Bragg's Liquid Aminos: An unfermented soy sauce substitute made from soybeans and distilled water.

Barley Malt Syrup or Brown Rice Syrup: Both are thick rich syrups that can be used interchangeably with honey.

Carob Powder: A natural chocolate substitute. It is made from a locust bean pod that is naturally sweet and rich in calcium, phosphorus, magnesium, potassium and iron. Because of its natural sweetness, you will need to cut the sweetener in the recipe in half when replacing cocoa powder.

Carob Chips: Use in place of chocolate chips in any recipe. Be sure you are choosing one that is free of dairy and sweetened naturally with malted barley.

Coriander or Cardamom: Both spices found in any local grocery or health food store. When combined, they make a great substitute for cinnamon. (Cinnamon can be an irritating spice).

Instant Clearjel Powder: A thickening agent made from corn. It does not require cooking. Blend in blender with ingredients to thicken and prevent lumping.

Emes Kosher Jel: An all vegetable gelatin containing carrageenan, locust bean gum and cottonseed gum. Dissolves when heated and will gel as it cools. Available in plain or fruit flavors.

Emes Kosher Marshmallows: Made with all vegetable gelatin, and contains no dairy, available in regular or mini marshmallows.

Emes "Chicken-like" or "Beef-like" seasoning: All vegetable based, low sodium and contains no preservatives, artificial coloring or flavors.

ENER-G Egg Replacer: A non-dairy powdered leavening and binding agent used as a substitute for eggs in baked goods. It is made from tapioca flour, potato starch and leavening.

Flaxseed Jel: Used as an egg substitute for binding loaves or patties. Made from flaxseeds and water.

Insta-soy: Soymilk powder produced by "Cedar Lake Foods". Comes in powder form.

Mori Nu Silken Tofu: A smooth textured tofu made from soybeans. It is sealed in a Tetra Pak with a long date for easy storage, available in soft, firm or extra firm.

Nutritional Yeast Flakes: A good tasting yeast that is yellow in color and has a cheese-like flavor. "Red Star" brand is a good one because it is rich in B vitamins.

Sucanat: Made from organic sugar cane juice in granulated form. It is an unrefined product and retains all the vitamins and minerals provided by nature, an excellent substitute for white or brown sugar.

Tahini: A thick, smooth paste made from sesame seeds.

Tofu: Fresh soybean curd, white in color and easy to digest. Available in soft, medium, firm or extra firm textures.

TVP or Textured Vegetable Protein: A meat substitute made from defatted soy flour that is compressed until the protein fibers change in structure. Sold in dehydrated granular or chunk form.

MGM Foods: Imitation meat analogs. They contain no preservatives and are low in fat and sodium compared to other analogs.

• **"Golden Nuggets":** Breaded chicken flavored vegetable protein nuggets. Comes frozen in a vacuum pack.

• **"MGM burger":** Beef flavored vegetable protein. Ground meat texture. Comes in canned form.

• **"No Turkey":** Turkey flavored vegetable protein. Comes in a frozen roll or sliced in small packages.

Soy Milk Powder: Milk substitute made from soybeans. Comes in powdered form.

Tofu Milk Powder: Milk substitute made from tofu. Delicious tasting and comes in a powdered form.

Whole Wheat Pastry Flour: wonderful flour used for most baked goods such as muffins, cakes or cookies.

Breakfasts

Breakfast

We have all heard it before, and we need to hear it again... Breakfast is the most important meal of the day! When we wake up in the morning, our body has been fasting for about 12 hours or more. It needs fuel in order to work at peak efficiency. So now it is time to "break" the "fast".

Eating a good balanced breakfast will:

• Supply energy when we need it most

• Provide ⅓ to ½ of the total days nutritional requirements

• Help stabilize blood sugar levels

• Control weight by promoting regular meals

• Stop the urge to snack

• Prevent irritability fatigue

• Promote better attitudes and scholastic attainment

One should try to avoid the stereotyped breakfast, for knowing what will appear before them at every morning meal, come to dread the hour that should be interesting to them. Therefore it is important to prepare a variety of simple, healthful dishes to arouse the appetite.

"Blessed are you, oh land, whose princes eat at a proper time for strength and not for drunkenness." Ecclesiastes 10:17, NIV

APPLE TORTILLAS

FILLING:
8 apples peeled, cored and diced
1 c. water
¼ c. chopped dates
¼ c. raisins
¼ tsp. maple extract
½ tsp. vanilla
Place all ingredients in medium size saucepan and simmer until soft. Set aside.

TORTILLAS:
2 c. whole-wheat flour
½ c. unbleached white flour
¾ c. hot water
½ tsp. salt
¼ c. applesauce
Mix dry ingredients together. Add remaining ingredients and mix well. Divide dough into golf size balls. Roll each piece thin with rolling pin. Fry on a hot, non-stick frying pan each side until brown. Place on a plate covered with a damp cloth to keep each tortilla soft.

GLAZE:
3 c. apple juice
3 Tbsp. cornstarch
1 tsp. lemon juice
½ tsp. coriander } (You may replace these spices with
¼ tsp. cardamom } 1½ tsp. cinnamon)
Place all ingredients in a small saucepan. Simmer over medium heat until glaze thickens.

1. Place a thin layer of glaze in the bottom of a 9"x12" glass baking dish.
2. Place approximately ½ cup of apple filling in the center of each tortilla shell. Roll shell and place in baking dish seam side down. Repeat with each tortilla shell until finished.
3. Pour the remaining glaze over tortillas evenly.
4. Cover dish and bake in oven at 350 degrees F. for 30-40 minutes.

• This dish makes a delicious breakfast, dessert, or light supper.
• Freezes well once baked.

FRENCH TOAST

½ c. raw sunflower seeds
2½ c. water
2 Tbsp. liquid honey
1 Tbsp. maple extract
¼ tsp. sea salt
2 c. quick cooking oats
12 slices of whole-grain bread or as needed

1. Place all ingredients in blender and blend until smooth and creamy. Pour mixture into a flat dish or bowl.
2. Dip each slice of bread in mixture covering both sides. Place on a lightly greased cookie sheet and place in preheated 400 degrees F oven. Bake 10-15 minutes then flip each piece over and continue baking until golden brown.

• These freeze well and can be easily reheated in the toaster or microwave.

CASHEW OAT WAFFLES

2 c. water
½ c. raw cashews
½ c. soy or tofu milk powder
½ tsp. sea salt
1 Tbsp. honey
1 Tbsp. wheat germ
1 tsp. vanilla
3 Tbsp. oil
2 c. quick or rolled oats

1. Blend cashews in water until smooth in blender.
2. Add remaining ingredients then blend together.
3. Let mixture stand 5 minutes to thicken.
4. Cook approximately 7 minutes in hot waffle iron until golden brown.

• These freeze well and can be easily reheated in a toaster or microwave.

PINTO BEAN WAFFLES

2¼ c. water
1½ c. rolled oats
1 c. soaked pinto beans
1 Tbsp. oil
1 Tbsp. honey
½ tsp. sea salt

1. Combine all ingredients together in blender. Blend until light and fluffy. Let stand 5 minutes.
2. Again blend briefly. Bake in a preheated waffle iron approximately 8 minutes or until done.

SOYBEAN WAFFLES

½ c. soybeans
Water to cover soybeans
2½ c. water
1½ c. quick cooking oats
1 Tbsp. oil
½ tsp. sea salt
1 tsp. honey or Sucanat

1. Place soybeans in a bowl. Pour water into bowl until approximately 1-inch above soybeans. Allow soybeans to soak over night.
2. Drain remaining water off soybeans in the morning.
3. Place all ingredients in a blender and blend until very smooth.
4. Bake waffles in a preheated waffle iron for approximately 8 minutes or until golden brown.

• These waffles are amazingly light and fluffy.

WHOLE WHEAT PANCAKES

3 c. whole-wheat flour
3 tsp. baking powder (alum free)
½ tsp. sea salt
1 Tbsp. liquid honey or Sucanat
2 c. soy or tofu milk
3 Tbsp. oil
3 tsp. Egg Replacer powder dissolved in 4 Tbsp. water

1. Mix dry ingredients together.
2. Add remaining ingredients and stir gently until well mixed. Do not overmix.
3. Drop by spoonfuls on hot griddle. Fry until golden brown. Flip pancake and repeat process.

TOFU CREPES

1 (300 g.) package soft tofu
1½ c. soy or tofu milk
3 tsp. baking powder (no alum.)
2 Tbsp. honey
1½ c. flour
½ tsp. vanilla

1. Preheat a 6-inch non-stick frying pan.
2. Place all ingredients in a blender.
3. Blend until very smooth
4. Pour ⅓ cup batter into hot frying pan.
5. Fry until lightly browned on both sides.
6. Serve rolled with thickened fruit in the middle.

STRAWBERRY TOPPING

3 c. frozen strawberries
3 c. apple juice
3 Tbsp. cornstarch

1. Slice strawberries and thaw in medium saucepan at room temperature.
2. Combine ingredients. Bring to a boil over medium heat. Simmer until thick and clear.

• Use on waffles, pancakes, french toast, or as a topping for "cheesecake".

CREAMED PEARS

1 c. raw cashews
1 tsp. vanilla
1 Tbsp. liquid honey
2 (14 oz) canned pears, unsweetened

1. Drain juice off canned pears and reserve.
2. Place all ingredients into blender.
3. Blend until very smooth. Slowly pour juice reserved from pears into blender as needed until the desired consistency is reached.
Options: Substitute canned pears with canned peaches or frozen thawed strawberries.

HERBED POTATOES

4-6 medium potatoes
Olive oil
Sea salt
Fresh herbs such as: thyme, oregano, chives, etc.
(You may substitute Spike, Vegit, or Herbamere in place of fresh herbs)

1. Wash potatoes but do not peel. Cut each potato into 1-inch cubes.
2. Toss potatoes in a little olive oil and place in covered wok or fry pan.
3. Allow to steam for about 5 minutes. Remove lid and continue to fry until golden brown. Toss with herbs and cook for 1-2 minutes longer. Serve immediately.

- Serve with homemade ketchup *see recipe pg. 42

SCRAMBLED TOFU

1 Pkg. medium/firm tofu
½ tsp. garlic powder
½ tsp. onion powder
1 Tbsp. parsley flakes
3 Tbsp. Bragg's liquid aminos
1 Tbsp. Emes chicken-like seasoning
¼ - ½ tsp. paprika
Option: simulated bacon bits

1. Preheat a large nonstick frying pan.
2. Drain and rinse tofu. Chop and mash with spoon into frying pan.
3. Sprinkle all seasonings equally over tofu. Mix well. Add "bacon bits: if desired or sprinkle over mixture before serving if you wish for them to remain crunchy.
4. Stir occasionally; cook until most of moisture has disappeared. Serve fresh and hot.
Option: you may sautè onion, mushrooms, peppers, etc. before adding tofu.

APPLE'S N' RICE

2 c. cooked brown rice
1 medium apple cored, peeled and chopped
⅓ c. unsweetened apple juice
¼ c. pure maple syrup
1 Tbsp. lemon juice
½ tsp. cinnamon

1. Combine all ingredients in casserole dish. Cover.
2. Bake at 350 degrees F. for 45 minutes.

GRANOLA

13 c. quick oats or old fashioned rolled oats
1½ c. unsweetened shredded coconut
½ c. Sucanat sugar
2 c. sliced almonds
2 c. wheat germ
½ Tbsp. sea salt
1 c. sunflower seeds
½ c. brown sesame seeds
1 c. water
¾ c. oil
1½ Tbsp. vanilla extract
1 Tbsp. maple extract
1 Tbsp. raisins
1 Tbsp. chopped dates

1. Mix together dry ingredients except raisins and dates in a large bowl.
2. Stir together water, oil, vanilla and maple extracts. Pour over dry mixture and mix very well.
3. Spread granola ½-inch thick over a cookie sheet. Bake in oven at 350 degrees F. until golden brown. Stir approximately every 5-10 minutes.
4. Remove from oven. Mix in raisins and dates.
5. Store in an airtight container to retain freshness.

BREAKFAST TOFU DRINK

1 can frozen unsweetened orange juice
1 Pkg. soft tofu
1 banana or a few strawberries

1. Thaw orange juice, place in blender with tofu, banana or strawberries. Blend until smooth.
2. Drink immediately. Keep leftovers in refrigerator.

Breads

Bread Making

Whole-wheat flour is very nutritious.

So-called "enriched flour" has most of the food value removed and only one -sixth replaced.

When wheat is milled into bleached flour we lose:

- 30% of the protein
- 92.7% of the cellulose
- 59.4% of the calcium
- 50% of the copper
- 92.5% of the manganese
- 86% of the B1
- 41% of the fat (this is good fat your body requires)
- 84.9% of the iron

When you realize how much nutrition is lost, how "enriched" do you feel?

The following are a few tips for successful bread making:

1. Try a simple basic recipe first.
2. Salt and fat both slow the growth of the yeast and should not be added to the yeast mixture until it has grown strong and lively by feeding on sugar and starch. (Too much sugar can also slow the growth)
3. Develop the gluten of the wheat-flour in the batter by beating thoroughly before adding other kinds of flour.
4. It is important to do a thorough job of kneading before the first rising.
5. Never fill pans too full. Give the bread enough room to expand without having to billow out over the sides, causing cracked, over-browned crusts.
6. It is important each loaf is thoroughly baked. (It is better if the loaf is small rather than unbaked.
7. Careful not to "over-raise" breads when in loaf pans. Bake bread when loaf is approximately double in bulk.
8. Bread should slip easily out of pan if thoroughly baked.

- Bread just out of the oven is difficult to digest. Bread should be atleast 12 hours old before it is eaten.

- Bread freezes well.

- Use your imagination to make a wide variety of breads using different ingredients or combinations.

- Add 1 Tablespoon pure lemon juice for every 4 cups flour in the recipe to achieve a lighter, high-raising bread.

- Add 1 Tablespoon gluten flour for every 4 cups flour to make bread "less-crumbly" and raise nicer.

- Add 1 Tablespoon lecithin to make bread less crumbly.

COMMON DEFECTS OF BREAD AND POSSIBLE CAUSES:

DRY AND CRUMBLY: To much flour in dough.
: Over-baking.

HEAVINESS: Insufficient kneading.

CRACKS IN CRUST: Cooling in a draft.
: Baking before sufficiently light.
: Oven too hot at first.
: Yeast water too hot.

TO THICK A CRUST — DRY: Oven too slow.
: Baked too long.
: Excess of salt.

SOGGINESS: Too much liquid.
: Insufficient baking.

ILL-SHAPED LOAF: Not molded well originally.
: Too large a loaf for pan.

MULTIGRAIN BREAD

2 Tbsp. quick rise dry yeast
2½ c. warm water
⅓ c. liquid honey
2 tsp. sea salt
¼ c. oil
1 c. wheat germ
1c. raw sunflower seeds
1 c. either rolled oats, barley, spelt, or rye flakes.
½ c. sesame seeds
6 - 7 c. whole-wheat flour

1. Mix together yeast, water, honey, salt, oil, wheat germ, rolled grain of your choice, and seeds.
2. Begin adding 1 cup of flour at a time while mixing it in.
3. Add enough flour until dough is no longer sticky.
4. Let sit 10 minutes in a warm spot.
5. Knead by hand 10 minutes or approximately 5 minutes in mixing machine.
6. Shape into 2 loaves. Again let sit in a warm spot for ½ hour.
7. Bake 30 - 35 minutes at 350 degrees F. until crust in brown.

OATMEAL RAISIN BREAD

2 Tbsp. active dry yeast
½ c. warm water
2 c. hot water
¼ c. honey
½ Tbsp. sea salt
¼ c. oil
2½ c. quick oats
1 c. raisins
3 c. whole-wheat flour
3 c. unbleached white flour

1. Dissolve yeast in water and allow to activate. Set aside.
2. Combine hot water, honey, salt and oil. Cool to lukewarm.
3. Stir in oatmeal, raisins, and whole-wheat flour.
4. Stir in yeast.
5. Add remaining flour to make moderately stiff dough.
6. Turn dough out onto floured surface and knead until smooth.
7. Shape dough into ball and cover with towel. Let rise in a warm place for about 1 hour or until double in bulk.
8. Cut dough into 2 portions and shape each portion into a loaf. Place each loaf into a greased loaf pan and again cover with towel. Let rise about 1 hour or until double.
9. Bake at 350 degrees F. for 30-35 minutes or until golden brown.

100% WHOLE-WHEAT BREAD

2 Tbsp. dry yeast
½ c. warm water
⅓ c. honey
2 c. hot water
2 tsp. sea salt
¼ c. oil
1 c. wheat germ
6-7 c. whole-wheat flour

1. Mix honey in ½ cup warm water in a small bowl.
2. Add yeast to the water. Let sit approximately 10 minutes until yeast bubbles.
3. In a large bowl combine 2 cups warm water, salt, and oil. Stir in wheat germ and 3 cups flour.
4. Stir in yeast mixture. Mix well.
5. Add remaining flour 1 cup at a time kneading with hands. (you may wish to turn dough out onto a table or cupboard as you knead flour in)
6. Knead in enough flour until dough becomes smooth, non-sticky and forms a ball. (you may need a little less or more flour than what's called for)
7. Place dough in a lightly greased bowl. Cover with a clean dishtowel and let rise in a warm place until double in bulk. (approximately 1- 1½ hours)
8. Punch dough down. Cut dough in half. Form each half into a ball then shape into a loaf. Place each loaf in a greased loaf pan. Cover again and let rise another hour or until double in bulk.
9. Bake 30-35 minutes at 350 degrees F. until crust is brown.

REUBEN'S 100% WHOLE WHEAT BREAD

¼ c. oatmeal or quick oats
1½ c. whole-wheat flour
½ c. gluten flour
1 Tbsp. yeast
½ tsp. sea salt
⅓ c. date paste (in blender, blend dates with just enough water to make a paste)
1 Tbsp. unsweetened applesauce
3 c. very warm water (130 degrees F.)
5 - 6 c. whole-wheat flour

1. Stir together first 5 ingredients.
2. Add date paste, applesauce and water. Mix well about 200 strokes, until the consistency is like soupy, stringy pancake batter.
3. Add 5 - 6 cups of whole-wheat flour and mix thoroughly. Add enough flour so dough is not sticky or dry.
4. Let dough sit on a lightly floured surface for 5 minutes.
5. With your hands, knead for 10 minutes.
6. Shape dough into 2 loaves and place in lightly greased bread pans.
7. Cover with a clean dish towel and let rise 20 minutes.
8. Bake in a 350 degrees F. oven for 30 minutes or until the crust is golden brown.

POCKET BREAD

3 c. warm water
2 Tbsp. Fermipan yeast
2 Tbsp. liquid honey
½ c. unsweetened applesauce
1 Tbsp. sea salt
6 c. whole-wheat flour
2 c. unbleached white flour

1. Preheat oven to 550 degrees F.
2. In a large mixing bowl add water, yeast, honey, applesauce and salt. Stir well.
3. Mix in whole-wheat flour then add unbleached flour 1 cup at a time while kneading in with hands. Add enough flour until dough is no longer sticky. (You may need a little more or less than amount of flour called for)
4. Form dough into golf size balls or larger depending on the size you would like.
5. Roll with a rolling pin each ball until approximately ¼-inch thick.
6. Place on a dry cookie sheet. Raise for 10 minutes then place in hot oven. Bake 3-5 minutes until they "puff up" and become golden brown. Let bread cool.
7. Cut with a sharp knife half way around the side.
8. Stuff each pocket with your favorite fillings such as chili, fresh vegetables, mock tuna, tofu-egg salad, or serve with humus for dipping.

POTATO DOUGH

2 Tbsp. yeast
1 c. warm water
2 c. potato water (120 degrees F. approximately)
2 c. mashed potatoes
½ c. Sucanat
1 Tbsp. sea salt
2 Tbsp. oil
1 Tbsp. lemon juice
½ c. wheat germ
3 Tbsp. gluten flour
3 c. whole-wheat flour
3 c. unbleached white flour

1. Pour yeast in water and let sit 10 minutes or until yeast softens and begins to bubble.
2. In a large mixing bowl, measure and add Sucanat, salt, wheat germ, gluten flour, and whole wheat flour. Mix together. Add oil and lemon juice to potatoes then mash well and add to dry ingredients. Pour in warm potato water and yeast mixture. Mix well.
3. Add 3 cups unbleached white flour while kneading in with hands. Add enough flour until dough is no longer sticky. (Approximately 1 cup or more)
4. Cover and let rise in a warm place for about 1½ hrs.
5. Shape into buns and let rise another 30-40 minutes. Bake 25-35 minutes at 350 degrees F.

CORN BREAD

1 c. cornmeal uncooked
1½ tsp. baking powder (alum. free)
¼ tsp. sea salt
3 tsp. Egg Replacer powder
4 Tbsp. water
1 can cream style corn
¼ c. olive or safflower oil
1 (300 g.) Pkg. Soft tofu

1. Dissolve Egg Replacer powder in water.
2. Mash or blend in blender tofu until smooth.
3. Mix all ingredients together and pour into a lightly greased 8 X 8-inch pan.
4. Bake in 400 degrees F. oven for 25 minutes or until golden brown.
5. Serve with chili on top.

WESTERN BISCUITS

1 c. whole-wheat flour
1 c. unbleached white flour
3 tsp. baking powder (alum. free)
½ tsp. sea salt
¾ c. tofu or soy milk
4 Tbsp. vegan Canoleo margarine or ⅓ c. olive oil

1. Mix together flour, baking powder and salt.
2. Add oil or margarine and mix well with a fork.
3. Add soy or tofu milk slowly and mix to a soft dough.
4. Roll out on a slightly floured board to ½-inch thick.
5. Cut with a biscuit cutter.
6. Lay on a lightly greased cookie sheet.
7. Bake at 450 degrees F for 10 - 15 minutes. Serve warm.
Makes 12 biscuits

PITA CHIPS

1 Pkg. whole-wheat pitas
½ c. olive oil
2 tsp. garlic powder
1 tsp. Spike seasoning

1. Mix together in a small bowl olive oil and seasonings.
2. Cut each pita into 8 pieces, pie shape.
3. Using a pastry brush, brush the seasoned oil on both sides of each pita piece.
4. Place pita pieces on a cookie sheet. Bake in oven at 400 degrees F. until golden brown. (watch carefully- they burn quickly)
5. Let cool. Serve immediately as a "cracker" or "chip".

PIZZA BREAD

1 pizza crust *see recipe pg. 32
Olive oil
Oregano
Diced tomatoes
Fresh garlic cloves
Option: rice or soy parmesan cheese

1. Press pizza crust into a lightly greased pizza pan.
2. Using a pastry brush, brush a thin layer of olive oil over crust.
3. Sprinkle with oregano, tomatoes and garlic.
4. Bake at 350 degrees F. for 10 minutes.
5. Remove pizza bread from oven and sprinkle with rice or soy parmesan cheese if desired. Return to oven and continue baking until crust becomes golden brown.

TROPICAL SURPRISE MUFFINS

2 c. whole wheat pastry flour
½ c. unsweetened coconut
2 tsp. baking powder (alum. free)
½ tsp. sea salt
¾ c. soy or tofu milk
1½ tsp. Ener-G egg replacer dissolved in 2 Tbsp. water
¼ c. olive oil
½ c. liquid honey
1 tsp. vanilla extract
⅓ c. strawberry or raspberry jam *see recipe pg. 36

1. In a bowl, mix together all ingredients except jam.
2. Fill each lightly greased muffin tin ⅓ full.
3. Place 1 tsp. of jam on each muffin, then top with dough until ⅔ full.
4. Bake at 350 degrees F about 20 minutes or until golden brown.

• Makes 1 dozen

HOMEMADE PIZZA

Crust:
2 c. whole-wheat flour
1 Tbsp. Fermipan yeast
1 Tbsp. honey
¾ c. water
½ tsp. sea salt

Sauce:
½ c. tomato sauce
½ tsp. garlic powder
½ tsp. oregano

Topping:
1 medium onion, sliced
½ green pepper, sliced
6 - 8 fresh mushrooms, sliced
1 small can pineapple tidbits, drained
½ c. black olives, sliced
½ c. dry TVP beef-like granules rehydrated, or 1 roll MGM Vege-Pizza
Topping, sliced
1 - 2 c. soy, tofu or rice cheese, grated
1 medium tomato, sliced

1. Mix together 1 cup flour, salt, yeast, honey and water.
2. Add last cup of flour and mix until dough forms a nice ball (if dough is sticky, add a dash more flour).
3. Place dough ball in center of a lightly greased pizza pan.
4. Cover with a clean dishtowel and let sit for 10 - 15 minutes.
5. Press into pizza pan and about ½-inch up sides all around.
6. Mix together tomato sauces with seasonings.
7. Spread evenly over pizza dough.
8. Layer on pizza toppings: Cedar Lake TVP granules or MGM Vege-Pizza Topping, onions, mushrooms, olives, pineapple bits, green pepper, then soy/tofu/rice cheese.
9. Bake in a 350 degrees F. oven until crust is brown and bottom is done. (Check bottom using a spatula).
10. Remove from oven and place fresh sliced tomatoes evenly over the top.
Option: sprinkle with oregano for garnish. Slice into eight pieces.

OAT CRACKERS

3 c. quick oats
2 c. unbleached white flour
1 c. wheat germ
2 Tbsp. liquid honey
½ tsp. sea salt
¾ c. oil
1 c. water

1. Mix all ingredients together.
2. Roll dough out on a cookie sheet using a rolling pin keeping equal thickness throughout pan. (For thinner crackers, divide dough between two cookie sheets)
3. Cut dough into desired shape with a sharp knife, pizza cutter or cookie cutters.
4. Sprinkle with sea salt if desired.
5. Bake at 325 degrees F. for about 30 minutes or until golden brown.

SWEET ROLLS

1 Recipe bread dough (pan stage)
Pure maple syrup
Cinnamon or ½ tsp. cardamom and ½ tsp. coriander
1 large or 2 small apples peeled, cored and chopped
Raisins
Dried cranberries
Pecan pieces

1. Roll bread dough out to ¼-inch thickness or less.
2. Pour maple syrup in center of dough. Spread around with knife. (use enough to make a thin layer over dough)
3. Sprinkle with cinnamon or cardamom and coriander.
4. Sprinkle chopped apples, raisins, cranberries and pecans over dough.
5. Roll up as you would cinnamon rolls. Slice each piece approximately ½-inch thick.
6. Coat each slice in maple syrup on counter that ran out of dough. Place flat side down in a lightly greased pan or large muffin tins.
7. Cover pan with towel and let raise minimum 20 minutes, (depending on bread recipe), or until approximately double in bulk.
8. Place pans in preheated oven at 350 degrees F. until golden brown.

Spreads, Sauces, and Gravies

"An alarming increase in crime and disease has succeeded in every generation. Intemperance in eating and drinking, and the indulgence of the baser passions, have benumbed the nobler faculties of man. Reason, instead of being the ruler, man has come to the being of slavery towards appetite at an alarming rate. Increasing desire for rich foods has been indulged, until it has been the becoming fashion to crowd all the delicacies possible into the stomach. Especially at parties the appetite is indulged with but little restraint. Rich dinners and late suppers are served, consisting of highly seasoned meats, with rich sauces, cakes, pies, ices, teas, coffee, etc. No wonder that, with such a diet, people have allow complexions, and suffer from untold agonies from dyspepsia." Counsels on Diet and Foods, page 149.

STRAWBERRY JAM

2 c. frozen unsweetened strawberries
40 dried pineapple tidbits or 5 rings

1. Cut pineapple into pieces if using rings. Place pineapple in bowl.
2. Place frozen strawberries over dried pineapple and allow to thaw at room temperature for a couple hours.
3. Place mixture in food processor and blend until smooth and creamy.
4. Allow jam to set up in fridge, or use immediately as a topping for waffles, french toast or pancakes.

APRICOT JAM

1 c. dried apricots
Pineapple juice

1. Place dried apricots in a small bowl.
2. Pour enough pineapple juice in bowl to cover apricots.
3. Allow apricots to soak in juice 2-3 hours or until they become soft.
4. Place mixture in food processor. Blend until smooth and creamy. (Add a small amount of pineapple juice to processor if needed for blending.)
5. Chill jam before serving.

MOCK CREAM CHEESE

1 Tbsp. Kosher-jel Plain or powdered agar agar
¼ c. water
¼ c. boiling water
½ c. raw cashew pieces
1 tsp. sea salt
1 Tbsp. lemon juice
½ (454g) Pkg. medium/firm tofu
*opt. ¼ tsp. onion powder
* opt. green onions, chopped

1. Place jel in blender. Add ¼ cup water. Let sit 5 minutes.
2. Pour in boiling water. Whiz 30 seconds in blender.
3. Add remaining ingredients except green onions. Blend until mixture is very smooth.
4. Stir in green onions if desired. Pour into container or mold and refrigerate until set.
5. Spread on bagels, bread, or use in various recipes.

BETTER THAN BUTTER

1 c. cooked cornmeal, ¼ c. cornmeal simmered in 1 cup water until soft
¼ c. unsweetened coconut
½ tsp. sea salt
½ c. water
1 Tbsp. nutritional yeast flakes

1. Place all ingredients into a blender. (Hot or warm cornmeal works best).
2. Blend until very creamy and smooth.
3. Pour into a container or bowl. Cover. Place in fridge to chill. Butter will set up in fridge.

Options: to make "garlic butter" add:
1 tsp. garlic powder or 1 - 2 fresh garlic cloves
1 Tbsp. parsley flakes
(Butter bread and toast in oven to make garlic toast).

Options: to make "sweet butter" add:
¼ c. pure maple syrup and decrease water to ⅓ cup instead of ½ cup
(Use on pancakes or waffles).

• Cooked millet can be used in place of cornmeal if sensitive to corn.

MOCK TUNA

1½ c. cooked chickpeas, mashed
2 tsp. Bragg's liquid aminos
½ c. fresh parsley
4 green onions, chopped fine
½ c. tofu mayonnaise *see recipe on pg. 39 or use Nasoya Nayonaise
Pinch of sea salt
¼ c. nutritional yeast flakes
½ green pepper, diced fine
1 c. celery, diced fine

1. Mix ingredients together well.
2. Chill in refrigerator. Serve in sandwiches with lettuce or use on crackers or rice cakes.

BEAN SPREAD

2 c. cooked kidney beans
¾ c. celery, finely chopped
½ tsp. sea salt
¾ tsp. onion powder
¼ tsp. garlic powder
¼ c. onion, finely chopped
Option: ¼ c. grated soy cheese
⅔ c. tofu mayonnaise *see recipe on pg. 39

1. Mash or place in food processor cooked kidney beans. (Make as smooth as possible).
2. Mix in remaining ingredients.
3. Cover bowl and place in fridge. This makes a delicious sandwich spread, or use on crackers.

HUMUS

2 c. cooked chickpeas
⅓ c. tahini
¼ c. lemon juice
2 garlic cloves
Option: 1 tsp. Spike seasoning, salt-free, or dry dill
Sea salt to taste

1. Combine all ingredients in a food processor.
2. Blend until very smooth.
3. Add more lemon juice, garlic, spike or salt if needed to taste.
4. Serve as a dip for pita bread or use as a sandwich spread for open-face buns.

TAHINI BUTTER

2 c. brown sesame seeds
¼ - ⅓ c. olive oil

1. Place sesame seeds in blender or food chopper. Blend until seeds turn to a fine powder.
2. While blending, slowly add oil until mixture reaches a "peanut butter" consistency. Keep refrigerated.

TAHINI DRESSING

1 c. tahini (sesame seed paste)
¼ c. lemon juice
2 - 3 fresh garlic cloves
½ tsp. sea salt
¼ c. water

1. Place all ingredients in blender or food processor. Blend until very smooth.
2. Serve over falafels.

TOFU SOUR CREAM

1 (454 g.) Pkg. medium/firm tofu
1 c. raw cashews
½ - ¾ c. water
1 Tbsp. seasoning salt
½ tsp. garlic powder
½ tsp. onion powder
¼ c. lemon juice

1. Place all ingredients into blender.
2. Blend until very smooth. Chill a few hours before serving to enhance flavors.

TOFU MAYONNAISE

1 (454 g.) pkg. medium/firm tofu
1 c. cashews
⅓ c. water
¼ c. lemon juice
½ tsp. onion powder
1 tsp. garlic powder
½ tsp. sea salt
Option: 1 Tbsp. dry dill

1. Place all ingredients into blender. Blend until very smooth.
2. Allow to set and chill in fridge.
3. Use on sandwiches, burgers, or on salads or as veggie dip.

TARTER SAUCE

1 c. Tofu Mayonnaise *see recipe pg. 39
1 Tbsp. pickle relish
1-2 pickles, diced small
1 Tbsp. mustard
1 Tbsp. minced parsley
2 Tbsp. lemon juice

1. Blend together all ingredients thoroughly. Chill 1 hour in fridge before serving.
2. Serve with "mock fish sticks" or use on veggie burgers or tofu dogs. Will keep 1 week in refrigerator.

TOFU COTTAGE CHEESE

1 (454 g.) Pkg. medium/firm tofu
¾ c. raw cashew pieces
¼ c. water
1½ Tbsp. pure lemon juice
¾ tsp. garlic salt
½ tsp. onion powder

1. In a bowl mash tofu with fork. Place remaining ingredients in blender or food processor. Blend until smooth. Pour blended mixture over mashed tofu and mix well. Chill and serve.
NOTE: Works excellent in recipes to replace dairy cottage cheese such as lasagna.

"CHICKEN" GRAVY

⅓ c. oil
½ c. unbleached white-flour or brown rice flour
4 c. water
3 Tbsp. chicken-like seasoning
2 Tbsp. Bragg's liquid aminos
Sea salt to taste

1. In a saucepan, mix oil and flour together.
2. Whisk in water slowly and add seasoning. Bring to a boil then simmer until thickened.

"BEEF" GRAVY

⅓ c. oil
½ c. unbleached white flour or brown rice flour
4 c. water
3 Tbsp. beef-like seasoning
2 Tbsp. Bragg's liquid aminos
Sea salt to taste

1. In a saucepan, mix oil and flour together.
2. Whisk in water slowly and add seasonings. Bring to a boil then simmer until thickened.

CHEESE SAUCE

2 c. water
¼ c. chopped pimento (unpickled), or roasted red peppers
2 Tbsp. nutritional yeast flakes
1 tsp. sea salt
½ tsp. onion powder
¼ tsp. garlic powder
3 Tbsp. cornstarch
1 c. raw cashews
1½ Tbsp. lemon juice
Option: cayenne pepper or fresh jalapeno peppers chopped fine

1. Place all ingredients in blender except fresh pepper and blend until smooth.
2. Pour mixture into a saucepan. Add fresh, chopped pepper.
3. Cook over medium heat, stirring constantly until mixture becomes thick.
4. Serve warm over steamed broccoli or corn chips topped with fresh diced tomatoes, chopped green onions, and sliced black olives.

ALFREDO SAUCE

¾ c. cashews
1¼ c. water
1 Tbsp. unbleached white flour
1 Tbsp. chicken-like seasoning
½ tsp. sea salt
½ tsp. oregano
1 tsp. dry parsley

1. Place all ingredients except parsley, in a blender. Blend until smooth and creamy. Pour into a non-stick saucepan.
2. Stir in dry parsley.
3. Simmer over medium heat until sauce thickens.
4. Toss with fettuccine noodles. Serve immediately.

KETCHUP

1 c. tomato sauce
1 (5.5 oz.) can tomato paste
2 Tbsp. lemon juice
1 Tbsp. liquid honey
½ tsp. basil
¾ tsp. garlic powder
1 tsp. onion powder
¼ tsp. sea salt

1. Combine all ingredients. Stir well.
2. Chill in fridge. (freezes well)

GUACAMOLE

1 large ripe avocado
2 Tbsp. lemon juice
1 tsp. garlic powder
½ tsp. onion powder
½ tsp. sea salt

1. Cut the avocado in half and remove the pit. Remove avocado from skin using a spoon.
2. Mash avocado in food processor until smooth.
3. Add remaining ingredients, blend or mix well.
4. Serve immediately; as guacamole sits exposed to air, it will turn brown in color. Serve as a dip for nachos or use on taco salad, tacos, burritos, or haystacks.

SLICEABLE CHEESE

1 medium potato (1 cup diced)
1 medium carrot (½ cup sliced)
1 small onion (½ cup chopped)
½ c. liquid (liquid off cooking vegetables and water)
3 Tbsp. lemon juice
¾ c. raw cashew pieces
1 tsp. paprika
4 Tbsp. nutritional yeast flakes
1½ tsp. sea salt
½ tsp. garlic powder
1 Pkg. extra-firm Mori-Nu tofu
¾ c. water
4 Tbsp. Kosher Jel Plain or powdered agar-agar

1. Cook potato, carrot and onion in a little water until soft.
2. Drain liquid off cooked vegetables into measuring cup. Add water to make liquid an amount of ½ cup.
3. Place cooked vegetables, ½ cup liquid, lemon juice, cashews, seasonings and tofu in blender. Blend until very smooth.
4. Bring 1 cup of water to a boil. Remove from heat. Dissolve kosher jel or agar-agar in water. Add to blender. Blend until well blended.
5. Pour mixture into containers or mould. Chill in refrigerator until firm.

• Freezes well.

Main Dishes

The recommended daily protein intake is 46 grams a day for the average woman and 56 grams a day for the average man. The average non-vegetarian person consumes over 100 grams of protein per day. The kidneys and liver are then over-worked by trying to breakdown the high quantity of protein. The higher the intake of protein consumed, the higher the amount of calcium is excreted into the urine. This can lead to a loss in bone density and possibly osteoporosis. A vegetarian diet will supply more than ample amount of protein required. Food such as beans, peas, vegetables, and whole grain breads are excellent sources of protein without the added fat and cholesterol.

Did you know?

• Cholesterol is found in only animal products.
• Animal products contain only pure saturated fat
• Plants have only a small percent saturated fat; only the amount your body requires.

Vegetarians are able to enjoy a longer, healthier life. They are at lower risk for heart disease, cancer, diabetes, high blood pressure and obesity.

"Grains, fruits, nuts, and vegetables constitute the diet chosen for us by our Creator. These foods, prepared in a simple and natural a manner as possible, are the most healthful and nourishing. They impart strength, a power of endurance, and vigor of intellect, that are not afforded by a more complex and stimulating diet". Counsels on Diet & Foods, page 363.

NUT LOAF

2 c. raw cashews, ground
2 c. ground gluten*see recipe on pg. 54, or use prepared (MGM "Vegeburger" or Yves)
1 large onion, chopped
¼ c. celery, chopped
2 Tbsp. olive oil
1 c. bread crumbs (dry)
¾ c. tofu or soy milk
2 Tbsp. cornstarch or 3 Tbsp. arrowroot powder (heaping)
1 tsp. sea salt
1 Tbsp. Bragg's liquid aminos
2 Tbsp. chicken-like seasoning
1 Tbsp. dry parsley
1 tsp. poultry seasoning

1. Combine all ingredients and mix well.
2. Pour into 1 large or 2 small lightly greased loaf pans.
3. Bake at 350 degrees F. for 45- 60 minutes or until brown on top.
4. Remove from oven. Let sit 10 minutes before serving.
NOTE: Loaf is more stable if prepared the day before serving. Reheat loaf and tip onto a platter. Slice into ½-inch thick slices. Garnish with fresh parsley and cherry tomatoes.

SWEET N' SOUR TOFU ON RICE

1 green pepper, diced into 1-inch pieces
1 medium onion, diced into 1-inch pieces
2 c. celery, diced diagonally
2-3 Tbsp. olive oil or ¼ c. water
4 Tbsp. lemon juice
1 can pineapple tidbits and juice
1 (5.5 oz) can tomato paste
¼ c. Bragg's liquid aminos
1 Tbsp. honey or Sucanat
¼ tsp. garlic powder
¼ tsp. sea salt
1 Tbsp. cornstarch or 2 Tbsp. arrowroot powder
2 Tbsp. cold water
1 package extra firm tofu, or 1 small package MGM golden nuggets

1. In a wok or large pan, sautè green pepper, onion and celery in oil or water until clear.
2. Add lemon juice, pineapple and juice, tomato paste, liquid aminos, honey or Sucanat, garlic powder and sea salt.
3. Stir well. Dissolve cornstarch or arrowroot powder in 2 Tbsp. of water and add to pan.
4. Cook until sauce becomes clear.
5. Drain, rinse, and dice tofu into ½ - 1-inch cubes. Add to sauce.
6. Heat through. Serve over rice.

Option: Substitute MGM golden nuggets for the tofu and enjoy "sweet n' sour chicken".

VEGETABLE TOFU CREPES

Optional: Diced soy chicken
2 carrots, grated
3 c. chopped mixed vegetables, such as broccoli, cauliflower, celery,
green/red peppers, corn, peas, etc.
1 can mushrooms, drained or 6 fresh mushrooms, sliced
4 c. fresh bean sprouts
2 medium onions, chopped
Bragg's liquid aminos or soy sauce
⅔ c. green onions, chopped
1 c. whole-wheat flour or unbleached white flour
½ c. tofu, rice, or soy milk
¾ tsp. garlic powder
Dash of sea salt
1 pkg. medium firm tofu, drained
Grated soy or rice cheese

1. Dice soy chicken into 1-inch cubes.
2. Mix together in a large frying pan or wok: diced soy chicken, carrots,
   mixed vegetables, mushrooms, bean sprouts, and 1 onion.
3. Sautè to a soft desirable texture.
4. Add liquid aminos or soy sauce to taste then sautè slightly until most of
   the liquid has evaporated.
5. Set aside. Blend in blender flour, tofu/soy milk, garlic powder, salt and
   tofu until very smooth.
6. Stir in chopped green onions. Pour ¾ cup of batter into a small non-stick,
   preheated frying pan. Batter should be spread out evenly and to
   approximately ¼-inch thick over bottom of pan. Fry until bottom is
   brown, from pan when done.
7. Place approximately ¾ cup - 1 cup filling in center of crepe. Roll crepe
   around filling then place seam side down in a large baking dish. Once all
   the crepes have been completed in this way, sprinkle grated soy cheese
   over top.
8. Chop and sautè lightly 1 medium onion in olive oil, then pour over top of
   crepes.
9. Place dish in oven at 400 degrees F. to reheat and melt cheese. Makes
   approximately 10 crepes.

TOFU LASAGNA

1 lb. firm tofu, rinsed and drained
½ c. raw cashews
1 c. water
½ tsp. sea salt
1 Tbsp. nutritional yeast flakes
2 Tbsp. lemon juice
½ tsp. garlic powder
1 bunch fresh spinach
4 c. plain tomato sauce
1 tsp. basil
1 tsp. oregano
½ tsp. garlic powder
8 lasagna noodles, cooked
Fresh parsley for garnish

1. Lightly grease a 9 X 12-inch glass pan.
2. Layer lasagna noodles to cover bottom of pan over-lapping noodles slightly. Set aside.
3. In blender, blend tofu, cashews, water, salt, yeast flakes, lemon juice and garlic powder.
4. Spread ½ of tofu mixture evenly over noodles in baking dish. Layer some fresh spinach leaves over tofu mixture.
5. Whisk together tomato sauce, basil, oregano and garlic powder. Pour ½ of sauce over spinach.
6. Repeat another layer ending with tomato sauce. Sprinkle with fresh parsley.
7. Bake in 350 degrees F. oven until bubbling and done. Let sit for 10 minutes before serving.
• May be baked and frozen then reheated when desired.

HOMEMADE SPAGHETTI SAUCE

1 medium onion, chopped
2 c. ground homemade gluten burger*see recipe on pg. 54 or "Vegeburger"
(MGM or Yves)
1 c. mushrooms, sliced
2 Tbsp. olive oil
2 cloves garlic, minced
1 Tbsp. dry parsley
½ tsp. sea salt
Optional: green pepper, diced
1 (32 oz) can diced tomatoes
1 (6 oz) can tomato paste
1 (8 oz) can tomato sauce

1. In large pot or wok, sautè in olive oil, onion, "burger", mushrooms, and garlic until tender and slightly brown.
2. Add parsley, salt, green pepper, tomatoes, tomato paste and sauce.
3. Simmer for approximately 10 minutes then serve hot over spaghetti.

TOFU-MILLET BURGERS

1 (454g) Pkg medium/firm tofu
1 medium onion, chopped
2 c. quick oats
½ tsp. sea salt
½ c. millet cooked in 2 c. water until soft
½ c. pecans, ground
1 tsp. poultry seasoning
1 Tbsp. beef-like seasoning
¼ tsp. garlic powder
1 Tbsp. nutritional yeast flakes
2 Tbsp. Liquid Aminos

1. Blend tofu until smooth. Pour into mixing bowl.
2. Add remaining ingredients and mix well.
3. Drop by tablespoonfuls on a preheated non-stick skillet. Form into shape of a burger.
4. Fry both sides of burger until golden brown.
5. Serve warm on a bun with lettuce and tomato.

VEGETARIAN LASAGNA

1 Recipe Tofu cottage cheese *see recipe pg. 40
1 (28 oz) can diced tomatoes
1 (14 oz) can tomato soup, unsweetened
1 (5.5 oz) can tomato paste
1 Tbsp. honey or 2 Tbsp. Sucanat
2 c. Vegeburger (MGM or Yves)
1 bunch spinach chopped and lightly steamed
½ -1 tsp. sea salt
1 tsp. granulated garlic powder
1½ tsp. italian seasoning
½ tsp. oregano
¼ c. dried onion flakes
1 Tbsp. dried parsley flakes
12 lasagna noodles
soycheese

1. Cook lasagna noodles until tender or you may choose to use oven-ready noodles.
2. Prepare 1 recipe of tofu cottage cheese then set aside.
3. In a pot add remaining ingredients. Simmer 5 - 10 minutes until flavor is through.
4. Place a thin layer of sauce in the bottom of a 9 X 12-inch lasagna or baking dish.
5. Place 4 lasagna noodles, length-wise side by side over sauce.
6. Spread ½ of the remaining tomato sauce over the noodles.
7. Layer 4 more noodles over sauce.
8. Carefully spread cottage cheese over the noodles.
9. Layer the last 4 noodles over the cottage cheese.
10. Spread the last of the tomato sauce over the noodles.
11. Sprinkle with grated soy cheese.
12. Bake in a 350 degrees F. oven for about 30 - 45 minutes.
13. Let sit 10 minutes before cutting into squares and serve.

*Optional: Mix "cottage cheese" into tomato sauce.

LENTIL ROAST

2 c. cooked lentils
1 c. finely ground pecans
1¾ c. tofu or soy milk
1 small onion, chopped
¾ tsp. sea salt or 1 Tbsp. Bragg's liquid aminos
½ tsp. sage
½ tsp. garlic powder
1½ c. crushed Cornflakes (sweetened with fruit juice)

1. Mix all ingredients together well.
2. Pour into a lightly greased 9" casserole dish.
3. Bake at 350 degrees F. for 1 hour.

PASTA PRIMAVERA

2 c. fresh broccoli, chopped into bite size pieces
1 medium zucchini, diced into ½-inch cubes
¾ c. fresh snow peas
12 cherry tomatoes, halved or 1 large tomato chopped in coarse chunks
¼ c. fresh parsley, chopped
Olive oil
1 garlic clove, minced
2 c. fresh mushrooms, sliced
1 lb. or 500 g. linguini noodles, cooked (firm & tender)
⅓ c. rice or soy parmesan cheese
1 c. water
½ c. raw cashews pieces
1½ tsp. dried basil
Salt to taste

1. Sautè in olive oil, broccoli, zucchini, and snow peas about 3 minutes until tender-crisp.
2. Add garlic clove, parsley and mushrooms.
3. Heat through, then add tomatoes and sautè 3 - 5 minutes. Combine hot cooked pasta with vegetable mixture.
4. Blend cashews in water until very smooth. Pour over pasta.
5. Add salt, basil and rice or soy parmesan cheese. Toss lightly. Sprinkle lightly with more parmesan before serving.

GLUTEN

3 c. gluten flour
½ c. minute tapioca
½ c. whole-wheat flour
1 Tbsp. brewers yeast or 2 Tbsp. nutritional yeast flakes
2 Tbsp. beef-like seasoning
2 Tbsp. chicken-like seasoning
2¾ c. water
¼ c. Bragg's liquid aminos

Broth:
1 medium onion, chopped
10 c. water
1 (28 oz) can tomato sauce
2 Tbsp. beef-like seasoning
¼ c. Bragg's liquid aminos
1 tsp. instant coffee substitute
½ tsp. sea salt
½ tsp. Italian seasoning
½ tsp. garlic powder

1. In a large stockpot combine all ingredients for the broth. Bring to a boil then reduce to simmer or a slow boil.
2. In a large bowl combine gluten flour, tapioca, whole-wheat four, yeast and seasonings. Mix well. Make a well in the center. Pour in the liquid aminos and water. Mix altogether at once quickly. (You may need to use your hands). Shape into a roll.
3. With a sharp knife, slice so each piece is about ¼-inch thick.
4. Drop slices one at a time into the simmering broth. Gently stir the mixture occasionally. Place lid on pot and simmer for 1 hour to 1½ hours or until gluten pieces are desired texture. (The longer it boils, the tenderer it will become). When done, remove gluten from broth.
5. Dip in seasoned breadcrumbs. Fry both sides in a non-stick skillet with a little olive oil.

Seasoned Bread Crumbs:
1 c. fine bread crumbs • 2 Tbsp. nutritional yeast flakes • 1 Tbsp. parsley flakes • ½ tsp. garlic powder • ½ tsp. onion powder • ¼ tsp. paprika

Gluten freezes well. You may choose to grind up into burger or dice into cubes. The broth can be frozen and used again by just adding some additional water and/or tomato sauce. The following recipes will give you some ideas in preparing or using the gluten.

SWEET N' SOUR GLUTEN BALLS

1 recipe gluten and broth *see recipe pg. 54
3 Tbsp. cornstarch or arrowroot powder dissolved in a little cold water
1 can crushed pineapple with juice
1 (5.5 oz) can tomato paste
2 Tbsp. honey or Sucanat

1. Prepare recipe for gluten and broth as instructed.
2. Form gluten into golf-size balls then drop into boiling broth. Simmer gently for 45 minutes to one hour (until gluten is tender).
3. Remove balls from broth using a slotted spoon. Set aside in a serving dish.
4. Add remaining ingredients to broth. Simmer until clear and thick. (You may need to add more cornstarch or honey to sweeten). Stir constantly so it does not stick and burn.
5. Pour hot sauce over gluten balls. Serve with rice.

SHISHKABOBS

3 Gluten steaks cut into 1-inch cubes *see recipe pg. 54
3 pineapple rings cut into 1-inch chunks
12 cherry tomatoes
1 large green pepper cut into 1-inch pieces
1 large yellow pepper cut into 1-inch pieces
12 fresh mushrooms (if large, cut into halves)
1 c. Bragg's liquid aminos
¼ c. olive oil
1 Tbsp. honey or Sucanat
1 tsp. garlic powder
¼ tsp. ginger powder
¼ tsp. onion powder

1. In a bowl, measure out and mix together liquid aminos, oil and seasonings.
2. Place gluten cubes in liquid mixture and let marinate for about 10 - 12 hours (stir occasionally).
3. Place on a skewer one of each cherry tomato, pineapple, green pepper, gluten, yellow pepper, and mushroom. Repeat until skewer is full.
4. Lay skewer on cookie sheet. Repeat until all ingredients are used.
5. Pour a little marinating sauce over each skewer. (Not too much or it will burn on the cookie sheet).
6. Place in oven and bake at 400 degrees F for 10 - 15 minutes. Serve immediately.

MOCK GINGER - BEEF

3 c. gluten flour
⅓ c. minute tapioca
⅓ c. whole-wheat flour
½ tsp. sea salt
6 Tbsp. beef-like seasoning
2½ water
¼ c. Bragg's liquid aminos

Broth:
14 c. water • ¾ c. Bragg's liquid aminos • 2 Tbsp. olive oil •2 Tbsp. beef-like seasoning •2 tsp. ginger powder •4 tsp. garlic powder • ½ tsp. cayenne pepper

Coating:
2 c. unbleached white flour or whole-wheat pastry flour • 1 tsp. ginger powder • 2 Tbsp. nutritional yeast flakes • 1 tsp. paprika • ½ c. cornmeal
• Olive oil •Fresh ginger, minced • Fresh garlic cloves, minced
• 2 Tbsp. cornstarch • 1 Tbsp. brown sesame seeds

1. Mix thoroughly the first 5 ingredients. Make a well in the center and pour in water and liquid aminos. Mix together quickly.
2. Form dough into a log shape using your hands. Slice with a sharp knife so each piece measures ⅓ inch thick.
3. In a large pot, mix together all ingredients to make the broth. Bring to a boil then turn heat down to create a slow boil.
4. Slowly drop the pieces of gluten one at a time into the broth. Boil for about one hour.
5. Remove pieces of gluten from the broth using a slotted spoon.
6. Cut each piece into ½-inch strips.
7. Mix together flour, ginger powder, yeast flakes, paprika and cornmeal. Dip each strip of "gluten" into flour mixture.
8. In a large frying pan, heat olive oil with some minced garlic and ginger. Place floured gluten strips in frying pan. Brown each strip all the way around then place on a platter.
9. Dissolve cornstarch in little cold water. Add to left over broth. Cook over low heat until mixture thickens and becomes clear in color. (Add more water if too thick). Use this "gravy" to pour over "ginger-beef" before serving then sprinkle with sesame seeds.
Option: Instead of using "gravy" on gluten-strips, use to stir-fry vegetables as a side dish.

GLUTEN RICE CASSEROLE

2 c. cubed gluten *see recipe pg. 54
1 can pineapple tidbits, drained
1 can sliced mushrooms, drained
1 green pepper, chopped
2 tomatoes, diced
1 small head cabbage, shredded
3 - 4 carrots, grated
1 medium onion, chopped
½ Pkg. medium/firm tofu
8 c. cooked brown rice
2 c. frozen peas
Bragg's liquid aminos to taste

Sauce:
2 Tbsp. honey (liquid)
2 Tbsp. olive oil
4 Tbsp. lemon juice
½ c. Bragg's liquid aminos

1. In a small bowl, mix together ingredients for sauce. Mix in cubed gluten. Marinate for 1 - 2 hours.
2. In a large frying pan or wok, mash tofu and fry until liquid has evaporated.
3. Add cooked rice, peas and liquid aminos to taste. Fry until flavor is throughout rice. Place rice in a large baking dish.
4. In another small baking dish, mix together pineapple, mushrooms, peppers, tomatoes, gluten and sauce. Place in oven and broil for about 4 minutes.
5. Sautè in a little olive oil, cabbage and carrots for about 5 minutes. Layer over rice.
6. Pour vegetables, gluten and sauce over top of the casserole.
7. Place casserole in oven at 350 degrees F. until heated through. Serve with a salad.

GLUTEN PINWHEELS

1 pie crust recipe *see recipe pg. 123
2 c. ground gluten *see recipe pg. 54
½ tsp. garlic powder
½ tsp. onion powder
½ tsp. paprika
1 Tbsp. dry parsley flakes
3 c. mashed potatoes

1. Using wax paper, roll piecrust out into a rectangular shape and ¼-inch thick.
2. Spread evenly with hot mashed potatoes.
3. Mix seasonings evenly throughout ground gluten. Spread gluten over potatoes.
4. Roll dough lengthwise, snuggly across to the other side. (As if doing a cinnamon roll).
5. Cut with a sharp knife the "log" into ½-inch pieces. Lie each piece flat side down on a greased cookie sheet.
6. Bake at 350 degrees F. for about 30 minutes or until golden brown. Serve with gravy and cranberries. (Once baked, these freeze very well).

BAKED BROWN RICE

1 c. brown rice
2 c. water
½ tsp. sea salt
Option: substitute ¼ c. wild rice for ¼ c. brown rice.

1. Preheat oven to 350 degrees F.
2. Place water, rice and salt in a lightly greased baking dish.
3. Cover and bake in oven for 1 hour.

FRIED RICE

1 c. medium/firm tofu
4 c. cooked brown rice
6 fresh mushrooms, sliced
½ c. grated carrot
½ c. chopped green onion
2 Tbsp. chicken-like seasoning
Bragg's liquid aminos to taste

1. Mash and sautè tofu in a non-stick frying pan until most of the moisture has evaporated.
2. Add rice and remaining ingredients. Sautè until flavors are throughout and vegetables are tender.

MACARONI CASSEROLE

2 c. elbow noodles
4 c. water
1 tsp. sea salt
½ c. unbleached white flour
2½ c. water
½ tsp. sea salt
2 Tbsp. imitation bacon bits
1 c. grated soy cheese (or more if desired)
30 whole-wheat soda crackers
3 - 4 Tbsp. oil

1. Bring 4 cups of water to a boil. Add 2 cups of noodles and sea salt. Cook until tender. Drain and rinse in colander. Place in a lightly greased glass-baking dish.
2. In a small pot, whisk together, flour, 2½ cups of water and salt. Cook over low heat until thickened. Add grated soy cheese and bacon bits. Heat until melted. Pour over noodles and mix in well. Smooth top surface of pasta with back of spoon.
3. In a plastic bag, crush the crackers using a rolling pin. Pour into a small bowl and gently toss with oil. Sprinkle crumbs over top of casserole.
4. Place in oven at 400 degrees F. and bake for 12 - 20 minutes or until crumbs are golden brown.

BREAD DRESSING

4 c. fresh whole-wheat bread crumbs
¼ c. oil
½ c. water
¼ tsp. sea salt
1½ tsp. poultry seasoning
1 small onion, chopped fine

1. Combine all ingredients. Place in casserole dish. Cover.
2. Cook in microwave on high for 5 minutes. Stir. Microwave for 5 minutes longer or until onions are soft.
3. Serve. (You may bake in a 350 degrees F. oven until onions are tender instead of the microwave).

"TURKEY" AND DRESSING

½ MGM frozen "No Turkey" roll
1 recipe "Bread Dressing" *see recipe pg. 60
1 recipe "Chicken Gravy" *see recipe pg. 40

1. Cover bottom of a 9 X 12-inch baking pan with a thin layer of gravy approximately ¼-inch thick.
2. Slice turkey into round ¼-inch slices. Bend each slice of turkey into a "taco shell" shape. Fill with dressing and stand in baking dish. Repeat placing each "shell" snug against each other until the dish is full.
3. Divide remaining dressing evenly amongst each shell.
4. Drizzle gravy over top of turkey shells. Reserve remaining gravy to serve with meal.
5. Place dish in oven at 350 degrees F. until golden brown.
6. Serve with cranberries.

• When serving, each piece will hold its shape better, if baked a day in advance.

TOMATO COUSCOUS WITH CHICKPEAS

1½ c. water
2 Tbsp. chicken-like seasoning
½ tsp. sea salt
1½ c. couscous
1 Tbsp. olive oil
1 (28-oz.) can diced tomatoes
2 tsp. curry powder
1 clove garlic, minced
1 (19 oz.) can chickpeas, drained
½ c. fresh parsley, chopped
½ onion, diced

1. Drain juice off canned tomatoes into a saucepan. Add water, salt, and chicken-like seasoning. Bring to a boil.
2. Stir in couscous. Cover pan and remove from heat. Let sit 5 minutes.
3. In a large non-stick pan over medium heat, sautè in olive oil, onion and garlic until they become transparent.
4. Add tomatoes, curry powder, fresh parsley and chickpeas to pan. Sautè for approximately 5 minutes or until heated through.
5. In a large serving bowl, toss the chickpea mixture with the couscous.
6. Serve warm or cold as a salad.

CURRIED QUINOA WITH PINENUTS

2½ c. water
2 Tbsp. curry powder
½ tsp. salt
1½ c. Quinoa
1 Tbsp. olive oil
1 c. fresh mushrooms, sliced
1 small onion, chopped
½ c. fresh parsley, chopped
2-3 garlic cloves, minced
¼ tsp. ground cloves
½ red bell pepper, diced fine
¼ c. pine nuts, lightly roasted

1. Rinse quinoa grain in a mesh colander thoroughly.
2. Bring water to a boil in saucepan. Stir in 1 tablespoon of curry powder, salt and quinoa. Simmer 15 minutes.
3. Remove from heat, cover and let sit 5 minutes.
4. Heat oil in a large non-stick frying pan. Add remaining 1 tablespoon of curry powder, mushrooms, onion, parsley, garlic, cloves and red pepper. Sautè until onion turns clear in color.
5. Add mixture to cooked quinoa. Cook for a couple minutes over medium heat until liquid has evaporated.
6. Stir in pine nuts and serve.

VEGGIE FRANKS AND BEANS

2 c. white navy beans
6 c. water
1 onion, finely chopped
1 Tbsp. honey or Sucanat
2 Tbsp. mustard
1 Tbsp. molasses
1 can tomato paste
1 can tomato soup, unsweetened
1 tsp. garlic powder
Sea salt to taste
1-2 Tbsp. Bragg's liquid aminos
1 Pkg. tofu dogs, sliced ¼-inch thick

1. In a large pot, bring water to a boil and add beans. Turn burner off and let sit 1 hour covered.
2. Add onion. Simmer until beans are tender.
3. Add honey or Sucanat, mustard, molasses, tomato paste, tomato soup, garlic powder, liquid aminos, tofu dogs, and salt to taste.
4. Simmer 10-15 minutes longer to allow flavors to marinate through.

TOFU COBBLER

FILLING:
3 Tbsp. whole-wheat flour
1 tsp. thyme
½ tsp. sea salt
1 Tbsp. wheat germ
2 Tbsp. olive oil
1 Pkg. firm tofu, cubed
1 small turnip, cubed
2 carrots, peeled and diced
1 Tbsp. parsley flakes or ¼ c. fresh chopped parsley
1 medium onion, chopped
1 large potato, cubed
2 stalks celery, sliced
1 c. green beans or peas

SAUCE:
2 Tbsp. oil
½ c. flour
3 c. water
3 Tbsp. beef-like seasoning

BISCUIT:
2 c. whole-wheat pastry flour
½ tsp. sea salt
1½ c. tofu or soy milk
2 Tbsp. lemon juice
4 tsp. baking powder (alum. free)
2 Tbsp. vegan Canoleo margarine

1. Preheat oven to 375 degrees F.
2. In a medium bowl combine flour, wheat germ, thyme and salt.
3. Toss tofu in flour mixture then sautè in oil until brown. Place in a 11x14-inch baking pan.
4. Add turnip, carrots, parsley, onion, potato, celery, beans or peas. Set aside.
5. In a medium saucepan combine oil, flour, water and beef-like seasoning. Whisk until smooth. Cook over medium heat until sauce thickens.
6. Pour sauce over vegetable mixture in baking pan. Toss gently.
7. Cover dish and bake in oven for 45 minutes.
8. Combine Biscuit ingredients in a separate bowl. Mix well.
9. Remove dish from oven. Drop mixture by spoonfuls over top of casserole.
10. Heat oven to 400 degrees F. Return dish to oven and bake 15-20 minutes or until golden brown.

KIDNEY BEAN ROLL-UPS

2 c. cooked kidney beans
½ c. finely chopped onion
½ c. finely chopped green pepper
½ c. grated soy cheese
1 tsp. chili powder
Pinch sea salt
1 Recipe Western Biscuit Dough *see recipe pg. 30

1. Mash kidney beans in food processor.
2. Mix in remaining ingredients.
3. Roll out biscuit dough to ¼-inch thick.
4. Spread kidney bean mixture evenly over dough.
5. Roll dough up gently lengthwise, as if making cinnamon rolls. Cut with a sharp knife each slice about 1-inch thick. Place each slice flat side down on a lightly greased cookie sheet.
6. Bake at 350 degrees F. for 20-30 minutes or until golden brown.

CURRIED CHICK PEAS WITH ONIONS

2 Tbsp. olive oil
2 onions, thinly sliced
2 cloves garlic, minced
2 Tbsp. brown sesame seeds
1 Tbsp. curry powder (or to taste)
2 (16oz.) cans chickpeas
3 Tbsp. lemon juice
1 Tbsp. Bragg's liquid aminos
3 Tbsp. chopped fresh parsley
Sea salt to taste
Fresh cooked brown rice

1. Cook onion and garlic in oil in a large covered frying pan until soft.
2. Stir in sesame seeds and curry powder. Cook uncovered for a couple of minutes.
3. Drain chickpeas, reserving ½ cup liquid. Add chickpeas and liquid to pan. Cook stirring often over medium-heat until almost all liquid has evaporated.
4. Stir in lemon juice, liquid aminos and parsley. Season with sea salt or additional liquid aminos to taste. Cook 5 minutes longer.
5. Serve hot over rice.

TASTY BLACK BEAN BURGERS

2 Tbsp. olive oil or as needed for frying burgers
1 onion, finely chopped
2 cloves garlic, minced
Option: 1 tsp. cumin seeds
2 Tbsp. chopped fresh parsley
1 (12 oz.) can black beans
1⅓ c. fresh bread crumbs
1 Tbsp. Ener-G egg replacer powder
¼ tsp. chili powder
Sea salt

1. Sautè onion and garlic in oil until soft.
2. Add cumin seeds and cook for 3 minutes.
3. Remove from heat and stir in parsley and beans.
4. Pureé in food processor.
5. Stir in breadcrumbs and egg replacer. Mix well.
6. Season to taste with chili powder and salt.
7. Shape into burgers and fry in a little oil if needed. Fry each side about 4 minutes or until lightly brown.

• Serve in toasted warm hamburger buns.

LENTIL POTATO PATTIES

Oil
1 onion, chopped
½ tsp. sage or poultry seasoning
2 c. cooked lentils
2 c. cooked mashed potatoes
½ c. finely ground pecans
½ tsp. sea salt

1. Sautè onion and sage in a little water or oil until onion becomes clear and soft.
2. Mix together all ingredients.
3. Form into small patties and place on a lightly greased cookie sheet.
4. Bake at 350°F until golden brown. (Approximately 20 min.)

RIGATONI

1 medium onion, chopped
½ green pepper, chopped
1 medium zucchini, cubed
3 stalks celery, sliced
1 can sliced mushrooms, drained
1 c. rehydrated TVP
1 large can zesty Italian tomato sauce
1 can tomato paste
1 can stewed tomatoes
½ c. water
1 tsp. garlic powder
½ tsp. onion powder
1 tsp. italian seasoning
½ tsp. crushed basil
½ tsp. oregano
Rigatoni Noodles; cooked according to package directions

1. Sautè onion, green pepper, celery and zucchini until soft.
2. Mix together all ingredients except pasta and place in large casserole dish.
3. Bake sauce in oven at 350 degrees F. until hot.
4. Serve sauce over hot cooked Rigatoni noodles.

SHEPHERD'S PIE

Olive oil or water for frying if needed
½ c. chopped onion
½ c. chopped celery
1 garlic clove, minced
1 c. dry TVP burger rehydrated in 1 c. boiling water, or
2 c. ground gluten *see recipe pg. 54
1 c. frozen peas
1 (14oz) can diced tomatoes
1 c. shredded carrot
1 Tbsp. beef-like seasoning
2 Tbsp. liquid aminos
3 large potatoes
1 c. nut milk (you may use soy or tofu milk)
1 Tbsp. parsley flakes
1 tsp. sea salt
Paprika

1. Sautè in small amount of oil or water: onion, celery and garlic until soft.
2. Add rehydrated TVP or gluten, peas, tomatoes, carrot, beef seasoning and liquid aminos. Simmer for about 5 minutes.
3. Pour mixture into a large casserole dish.
4. Peel, dice, and cook potatoes. Mash potatoes with nut milk, dry parsley and sea salt.
5. Spread mashed potatoes over gluten mixture. Sprinkle with paprika for color.
6. Bake at 350 degrees F. for 30 minutes or until heated through.

VEGGIE FAJITAS

2 c. gluten cut into thin strips *see recipe pg. 54
Olive oil
2 garlic cloves, minced
1 c. carrots thinly sliced into strips
1 small red pepper, sliced into thin strips
1 small green pepper, sliced into thin strips
1 small orange or purple pepper, sliced into thin strips
1 small yellow pepper, sliced into thin strips
1 small yellow onion cut in half and sliced into thin strips
¼ c. Bragg's liquid aminos
1 Tbsp. cilantro or parsley, chopped fine
1 tsp. basil
Tofu sour cream *see recipe pg. 39
½ c. chopped green onion
8 whole-wheat spinach or sundried tomato tortillas warmed

1. In a large fry pan or wok, sautè in a little oil, gluten strips, and garlic for approximately 4 minutes. Add carrot strips, then peppers and onion.
2. Pour liquid aminos and seasonings over mixture. Simmer until most of liquid is absorbed, but do not overcook.
3. Place approximately 1 cup of mixture in the center of warm tortilla then roll.
4. Serve with tofu sour cream and garnish with green onion.

BEAN BURRITOS

1 Tbsp. oil
1 large onion, diced
½ tsp. oregano
1 tsp. ground cumin
1 (14½ oz.) can diced tomatoes
4 c. cooked pinto beans
½ tsp. sea salt or to taste
8-12 whole-wheat tortillas

1. Sautè onion in oil over medium heat until soft and clear.
2. Add oregano, cumin and tomatoes. Bring mixture to a boil.
3. Add pinto beans and heat through.
4. Remove half of bean mixture to a bowl and mash with potato masher. Return mashed mixture to pan and heat through.
5. Season to taste with sea salt.
6. Warm tortilla shells. Roll approximately ⅓-½ c. filling in each tortilla.

FALAFEL'S

½ c. chickpea juice from can or water from cooking
2 (14 oz.) cans or 3½ c. cooked chickpeas
1 c. cooked yellow split peas
⅓ c. brown sesame seeds
2 Tbsp. dehydrated onion flakes
2 garlic cloves, minced
3 Tbsp. Bragg's liquid aminos
Whole-wheat bread crumbs
¼ c. wheat germ
2 tsp. cumin
1 Tbsp. dry parsley flakes
1 tsp. sea salt
2 Tbsp. lemon juice

1. Blend until smooth in food processor or blender: chickpeas, ½ cup juice from chickpeas, split peas, and sesame seeds.
2. Mix together the remaining ingredients except breadcrumbs.
3. Add crumbs slowly while mixing. Stir in just enough crumbs so mixture will hold together.
4. With hands, roll mixture into balls 1½ inches in diameter. Arrange balls on a lightly greased cookie sheet and bake in a preheated oven at 400 degrees F. for 20-30 minutes. Turn occasionally during baking to brown evenly.
5. Serve in pita bread or as an appetizer with Tahini Sauce. *see recipe pg. 39

PECAN RICE PATTIES

1 c. finely chopped pecans
1 c. cooked brown rice
1 c. whole-wheat bread crumbs
1 Tbsp. soy flour
½ tsp. sea salt
1 Tbsp. dry parsley flakes
1 small onion, finely chopped
1 c. soy or tofu milk

1. Combine all ingredients.
2. Shape mixture into patties on a lightly greased baking sheet.
3. Bake in pre-heated oven at 350 degrees F. until golden brown, about 40-45 minutes.
4. Serve with "chicken" gravy *see recipe pg. 40

CHILI RICE'N WIENERS

1½ c. diagonally sliced tofu wieners
1 medium onion, sliced
1 (540 ml) can diced tomatoes
1½ c. cooked kidney beans
½ tsp. sea salt
1 tsp. chili powder
3 c. cooked brown rice

1. Sautè wieners and onion until golden brown.
2. Mix together all ingredients and place in a lightly greased casserole dish.
3. Cover dish and bake in oven at 350 degrees F. for 20 minutes or until heated through.

CANNELLONI

1 c. dry TVP rehydrated in 1 c. boiling water
1 onion, chopped
2 cloves garlic, minced
1 recipe tofu cottage cheese *see recipe pg. 40
½ c. soy or rice parmesan cheese
1 Tbsp. parsley flakes
2 c. chopped steamed spinach
4 c. tomato sauce
Italian seasoning, basil, oregano, etc.

1. Sautè until brown TVP, onion and garlic.
2. Add "cottage cheese", "parmesan cheese", parsley flakes and spinach.
3. In a separate bowl mix together tomato sauce with seasonings of your choice to taste.
4. Coat the bottom of a 9x12-inch glass-baking dish with tomato sauce.
5. Stuff filling into raw cannelloni noodles then place in sauce in baking dish. (Okay if noodles touch each other). Continue until filling is gone.
6. Pour remaining sauce over noodles and cover dish. Bake at 350 degrees F. for approximately 1 hour.

VEGETARIAN FISH STICKS

1 c. oatmeal cooked in 2 c. water
4 c. tofu cottage cheese *see recipe pg. 40
¾ c. flaxseed gel *see recipe pg. 77
1 c. whole-wheat cracker crumbs
½ tsp. sea salt
1 c. chopped onion
2 Tbsp. chicken-like seasoning
1 Tbsp. nutritional yeast flakes
1 c. finely crushed cracker or Cornflake crumbs (juice sweetened)
1 tsp. onion powder
¼ tsp. garlic powder
¼ tsp. sea salt (do not add if crackers are salted)
Tofu or soy milk

1. In a large bowl mix together cooked oats, "cottage cheese", flaxseed gel, cracker crumbs, salt, onion, seasoning and yeast flakes.
2. Spread mixture evenly over a greased baking pan or cookie sheet. Bake at 300 degrees F. for 45 minutes.
3. Cover and let sit in fridge overnight.
4. Slice mixture into 2x4-inch pieces.
5. Mix together in bowl, cracker or cereal crumbs, onion powder, garlic powder, and salt.
6. Dip each "fish" stick in tofu or soymilk, then into crumb mixture.
7. Cook "fish" in a lightly greased skillet over medium heat until golden brown on both sides.

• Serve with Tartar Sauce *see recipe pg. 40

DINNER ROAST AND VEGETABLES

1 small can Cedar Lake Dinner Steaks
2 carrots, chopped in 1-inch chunks
1 medium onion, diced in 1-inch chunks
1 stalk celery, chopped in ½-inch chunks
2 medium potatoes, chopped in 1-inch chunks
¼ c. water
¼ - ½ tsp. sea salt
½ c. peas

1. Place carrots, onion, celery and potatoes into a casserole dish. Sprinkle salt over vegetables.
2. Drain gravy off dinner steaks over vegetables. Cut steaks into 1-inch pieces then add to mixture. Rinse excess gravy from can into dish using ¼ cup water. Stir mixture well.
3. Cover with lid and bake in a 350 degrees F. oven until vegetables are tender. Approximately 30 minutes.

SPAGHETTI PIZZA

8-oz. (250 g.) spaghetti or angel hair cooked until tender but firm
1½ tsp. Ener-G egg replacer powder
2 Tbsp. water
¼ c. tofu or soy milk
Salt, sprinkle
1 (7 oz) can tomato sauce
1 tsp. oregano
1 tsp. basil
¼ tsp. garlic powder
1 c. grated soy or rice cheese (mozzarella)
1 small onion, chopped
1 c. homemade ground gluten, or prepared soy meat such as MGM
Vegeburger, or rehydrated TVP
6 fresh mushrooms, sliced
⅓ c. sliced black olives
½ green pepper, diced
Option ½ c. diced unsweetened pineapple

1. Lightly grease a 12-inch pizza pan.
2. Mix egg replacer powder in water until dissolved. Add tofu/soy milk and salt. Stir in spaghetti noodles.
3. Pack into pan, raising edges slightly.
4. In small bowl mix tomato sauce, oregano, basil, and garlic powder together. Spread over noodles.
5. Layer onion, Vegeburger, mushroom, olives, green pepper, and pineapple over sauce.
6. Sprinkle with grated soy cheese.
7. Cover pizza with foil and bake in 350 degrees F. oven for 20 minutes. Remove foil and bake for 10 minutes more.
8. Cut into 8 wedges and serve.

SPAGHETTI PIE

CRUST:
6 oz (170 g.) spaghetti, cooked (tender and firm)
3 tsp. Ener-G egg replacer powder
4 Tbsp. water
⅓ c. grated soy, tofu or rice cheese

FILLING:
1 c. tofu cottage cheese *see recipe pg. 40
1 Tbsp. olive oil
2 c. ground gluten or prepared soy meat (MGM frozen burger or Yves)
1 small onion, chopped
½ green pepper, chopped
1 c. fresh mushroom, sliced
1 c. diced canned tomatoes
1 (5 oz) can tomato paste
1 tsp. honey
1 tsp. oregano
¼ tsp. sea salt
¼ tsp. garlic powder
1 c. gated soy or rice cheese (mozzarella)

1. Mix together egg replacer powder in water.
2. Add grated cheese and spaghetti noodles.
3. Shape into crust in a lightly greased 10-inch pie plate.
4. Spread "cottage cheese" over spaghetti crust.
5. Sautè in olive oil, onions, green pepper, mushrooms and burger until soft.
6. Add diced tomatoes, tomato paste, honey, salt, oregano and garlic powder. Mix together. Pour over "cottage cheese".
7. Bake uncovered in 350 degrees F. oven for 30 minutes. Sprinkle with soy cheese. Bake until cheese is melted. Cut into 8 wedges and serve.

COOKED LENTILS

3 cups water
1 cup lentils
1 medium onion, chopped
1 can tomato soup, unsweetened
½ tsp. garlic powder
sea salt to taste

1. Combine water, lentils, onion, garlic powder and salt in a pot. Simmer until lentils are slightly tender.
2. Add tomato soup and continue to simmer until lentils are cooked but not mushy.

• Excellent served over rice.

RICE STACKS

Cooked brown rice
Cooked lentils *see recipe pg. 75
Chopped lettuce
Chopped tomatoes
Diced cucumber
Chopped green onion
Sliced black olives
Grated soy cheese
Guacamole *see recipe pg. 43
Tofu sour cream *see recipe pg. 39

1. Serve each ingredient in separate bowls. (Rice and lentils to be served warm)
2. Individually build your own "stack" in the order of ingredients listed.

LENTIL TOFU QUICHE

½ c. dried green/brown lentils
½ tsp. sage
1 Tbsp. oil
1 medium onion, chopped
2 cloves garlic, minced
1 Tbsp. lemon juice
2 Tbsp. Ener-G egg replacer powder
1 c. soy milk
1 Pkg. soft tofu
½ tsp. sea salt
1 tsp. dried basil
1 tsp. oregano
½ c. unbleached white-flour
½ tsp. baking powder (alum. free)
½ c. soy cheese
2 Roma tomatoes, thinly sliced
1 Tbsp. Rice parmesan cheese

1. Rinse lentils. Place in medium saucepan with 2 cups water and sage. Simmer covered 25 minutes. Drain.
2. In a skillet, sautè onions and garlic until tender. Remove from heat and add lemon juice.
3. Place in blender egg replacer, soymilk, tofu, salt, basil, oregano and flour. Blend until smooth. Stir in baking powder, cheese, onions, and lentils.
4. Pour mixture into a lightly greased, 9-inch round casserole dish.
5. Lay sliced tomatoes over the top of mixture, then sprinkle with "parmesan" cheese.
6. Bake at 425 degrees F. for 45 minutes or until center is firm when pressed.

MEXICAN LENTIL CASSEROLE

2 Tbsp. Oil
1 medium onion, chopped
1 garlic clove, minced
1 medium green pepper, chopped
3 stalks celery, chopped
4 c. water
1 c. dried green/brown lentils
1½ c. cooked brown rice
1 (5.5oz.) can tomato paste
1-(39ml.) taco seasoning mix
1 tsp. chili powder
½ c. crushed taco chips
½ c. grated "sliceable cheese" *see recipe pg. 43

1. In a large saucepan, sautè onions, garlic, green pepper and celery in oil over medium heat for 5 minutes.
2. Add water and bring to a boil. Stir in lentils. Cover, reduce heat and let simmer for 40 minutes. Do not drain.
3. In a lightly greased, medium sized casserole dish, combine lentils with other ingredients except taco chips and "cheese". Bake uncovered for 20 minutes at 350 degrees F.
4. Sprinkle taco chips and cheese on top. Bake another 5-10 minutes until cheese is melted.

FLAX SEED JEL

2 c. water
6 Tbsp. flax seeds

1. Bring water to a boil in medium saucepan.
2. Add flaxseeds. Boil for 5 minutes.
3. Remove from heat and immediately pour through strainer with a bowl underneath.
4. The jel caught in the bowl is to be used as an egg substitute in recipes for binding such as "meatloaf's" or patties. Use approximately ¼ cup for each egg called for in a recipe. This jel will keep for approximately 1 week in your refrigerator. It will smell sour when it has gone bad. You may either discard the flaxseeds or use in your bread recipes.

Vegetables

"I give you every seed-bearing plant on the face of all the whole earth and every tree that has fruit with seed in it. They will be yours for food."
Genesis 1:29 NIV

STIR FRY VEGETABLES

1 - 2 Tbsp. olive oil
⅓ c. water
2 garlic cloves, minced
½ green bell pepper, diced into 1-inch cubes
½ red pepper, diced into 1-inch cubes
2 carrots, sliced diagonally
2 stalks celery, sliced into 1-inch diagonal pieces
1½ c. cauliflower pieces
1 medium onion, diced into 1-inch cubes
1½ c. fresh broccoli
Baby corn
Option: 1 small can water chestnuts
½ c. fresh pea pods
2 c. bok choy sliced into 1-inch pieces
6 fresh mushrooms cut in quarters
2 Tbsp. chicken-like seasoning
Bragg's liquid aminos to taste

1. Preheat oil and water in large frying pan or wok.
2. Add minced garlic and carrots. Sautè 5 minutes.
3. Add remaining ingredients. Sautè without a cover or lid until moisture eva-
   porates and vegetables soften slightly but are still crisp. Serve immediately.

STUFFED BAKED POTATOES

8 medium potatoes
2 c. soy milk
1 tsp. garlic powder
1 tsp. onion powder
½ tsp. sea salt
1 Tbsp. parsley flakes
Option: 1 Tbsp. imitation bacon bits
Grated soy cheese
Paprika

1. Bake potatoes until done in microwave or oven. Let cool.
2. Cut each potato in half. Scoop the middle out of each half being careful
   to not puncture the skin. (Do not worry about getting al the potato out).
3. Place inside of potato into food processor. Add soymilk, garlic powder,
   onion powder, salt, parsley and bacon bits. Blend until smooth. Divide
   evenly amongst each potato, filling the skins.
4. Sprinkle with soy cheese and paprika.
5. Bake at 400 degrees F. until cheese is melted.

BAKED CARROTS

1 lb. carrots
½ c. thinly sliced onion
1 - 2 Tbsp. dried parsley flakes
¼ - ½ tsp. sea salt
¼ c. water

1. Wash, scrape and slice carrots. Place in a lightly greased casserole dish.
2. Add remaining ingredients and mix well. Add more water if needed to cover bottom of casserole dish.
3. Cover. Bake in oven at 375 degrees F. for about 30 minutes or until carrots are tender.

BAKED YAMS

2 medium yams
2 c. pineapple juice
2 Tbsp. cornstarch
¼ tsp. sea salt
1 (14 oz) can pineapple rings
6 - 10 cranberries

1. Peel and slice yam into ¼-inch thick rounds. Place in glass pan.
2. Cover bottom of pan with water (approx. ¼ - ½ cup). Cover dish and place in microwave or oven and cook until tender. (Microwave about 10 minutes on high).
3. In a small saucepan, dissolve cornstarch in pineapple juice and add salt. Bring to a boil over medium heat stirring often. Simmer until mixture becomes thick and turns clear in color.
4. Pour thickened mixture evenly over yams. Top with pineapple rings and cranberries.
5. Bake in oven at 350 degrees F. for about 30 minutes.

CHEEZIE CAULIFLOWER CASSEROLE

1 c. room temperature water
½ c. raw cashews
2 Tbsp. Clearjel powder
2 Tbsp. nutritional yeast flakes
¾ tsp. sea salt
½ tsp. onion powder
¼ tsp. garlic powder
1 Tbsp. lemon juice
¼ c. cooked carrots
½ c. chopped onion
¼ c. chopped celery
1 (14oz.) can diced tomatoes
½ tsp. basil
1 tsp. dry parsley
1 medium cauliflower or approximately 4 c. raw cauliflower
Option: Grated soy cheese

1. Place cauliflower pieces in a baking dish.
2. Blend cashews in water in a blender until smooth.
3. Add Clearjel, yeast flakes, salt, onion powder, garlic powder, lemon juice, and cooked carrots. Blend until smooth and thick.
4. Pour blended mixture over cauliflower.
5. Sautè onion and celery in tomatoes in a non-stick pan until soft. Mix in basil and parsley. Pour mixture into casserole and mix well.
6. Cover dish and bake in oven at 350 degrees F. for 30 minutes.
7. Remove cover, sprinkle with soy cheese and return to oven. Bake 10 more minutes.

RUTABAGA PUFF

1 large rutabaga
1½ tsp. Ener-G egg replacer powder dissolved in 2 Tbsp. water
½ c. applesauce
3/4 tsp. sea salt
1 c. whole-wheat bread crumbs
1 - 2 Tbsp. oil

1. Peel, cube and cook rutabaga until tender. Drain and mash.
2. Add egg replacer, applesauce, ½ cup breadcrumbs and sea salt. Mix well. Pour into a lightly greased casserole dish.
3. Combine remaining breadcrumbs with oil. Sprinkle over rutabaga mixture.
4. Bake uncovered at 350 degrees F. for 45 minutes or until golden brown on top.

SQUASH WITH ROMA TOMATOES

2 medium zucchini sliced length-wise in half then sliced into ¼ -inch thick slices
4 small yellow crook-necked squash sliced length-wise in half then sliced into ¼ -inch thick slices
3 Roma tomatoes sliced round ¼-inch thick
1 Tbsp. olive oil or water
1 tsp. oregano
½ tsp. garlic powder
¼ - ½ tsp. sea salt
¼ tsp. onion powder

1. Sautè until tender, zucchini, crookneck squash and tomatoes in olive oil or water.
2. Add seasonings and salt while cooking. Do not overcook. Serve immediately.

"Nearly all the members of the human family eat more than the system requires. This excess decays and becomes a putrid mass...If more food, even of a simple quality, is placed in the stomach than the living machinery requires, this surplus becomes a burden. The system makes desperate efforts to dispose of it, and this extra work causes a tired, weary feeling. Some who are continually eating call this all-gone feeling hunger, but it is caused by the overworked condition of the digestion organs."
 Counsels on Diet and Foods page 133

Salads & Dressings

BOK CHOY SALAD

1 large fresh bok choy
2 c. fresh mungbean sprouts
1 c. raw sunflower seeds
Option: Fresh pea pods, chopped
½ c. olive oil
2 Tbsp. lemon juice
1 Tbsp. pure maple syrup
½ tsp. garlic powder

1. Chop bok choy and place in a salad bowl.
2. Add bean sprouts, sunflower seeds, and chopped pea pods. Toss gently.
3. In a separate bowl, whisk together oil, lemon juice, maple syrup and garlic powder. Pour over salad and mix well.
4. Allow salad to marinate ½ hour in fridge before serving.

GREEK SALAD

¼ c. extra virgin olive oil
¼ c. water
¼ c. lemon juice
½ tsp. oregano
¼ tsp. thyme
¼ tsp. sea salt
1 lb. extra firm tofu cut into 1-inch cubes
3 medium ripe tomatoes, diced
1 English cucumber, diced
1 c. black pitted olives
1 red onion, sliced

1. Mix the first 6 ingredients together well.
2. Add tofu cubes and toss gently. Marinate approximately 2 - 3 hours in fridge.
3. Add remaining ingredients. Mix gently.
4. Let sit another ½ hour in the fridge before serving.

TABOULI SALAD

1¼ c. fine bulgar wheat
½ tsp. sea salt
1½ c. boiling water
1 large fresh tomato, diced
½ English cucumber, diced
½ green pepper, chopped
1 c. black olives, pitted
6 Tbsp. fresh chopped parsley
3 green onions, chopped

DRESSING:
3 Tbsp. olive oil
3 Tbsp. lemon juice
½ tsp. oregano
2 garlic cloves, minced

1. Mix salt and bulgar wheat together in salad bowl.
2. Pour boiling water over bulgar wheat and leave for 20 minutes.
3. In a separate bowl, mix together dressing ingredients then pour over bulgar wheat. Mix well. Place in refrigerator for a couple hours or until ready to serve.
4. Add tomato, cucumber, green pepper, parsley, green onion and olives. Serve immediately.

BEAN SALAD

1 can or 1 c. cooked yellow beans
1 can or 1 c. cooked green beans
1 can or 1 c. cooked kidney beans
1 can or 1 c. cooked garbanzo beans
½ c. finely diced green pepper
½ c. diced red pepper
½ c. diced celery
½ c. finely diced onion
⅓ c. lemon juice
3 Tbsp. olive oil
½ tsp. sea salt

1. Drain and rinse beans.
2. Place all ingredients together in bowl. Mix thoroughly.
3. Marinate in refrigerator several hours before serving.

COUSCOUS SALAD

4 c. water
½ tsp. sea salt
4 c. couscous
1 bunch green onions, chopped (include the white parts)
1 can sliced black olives
1 large tomato, diced
1 c. diced english cucumber
¾ c. olive oil
1 tsp. garlic powder
¼ c. lemon juice
½ tsp. sea salt

1. Bring water to a boil in a pot. Stir in couscous and salt.
2. Remove from heat and cover. Let stand 5 minutes.
3. Pour couscous into a large bowl. Loosen couscous with a fork.
4. Add chopped green onion, olives, tomato, and cucumber. Mix together.
5. In a separate container, mix together oil, garlic, lemon juice and salt until well blended. Pour over salad and toss well.
6. Chill and marinate in fridge about one hour before serving.

• Prepare salad the same day it is to be eaten; otherwise vegetables will not remain crisp and fresh.

BLACK BEAN SALAD

1 can black beans, drained and rinsed
1 fresh bunch spinach
1 large tomato diced (yellow if in season)
1 Pkg. bite size corn chips
½ c. grated soy cheese
½ c. chopped white or yellow onion
½ c. Taco flavored TVP, rehydrated (¼ c. dry)
1 avocado, peeled and diced
Thousand Island salad dressing *see recipe pg. 91

1. Toss all ingredients together well.
2. Serve fresh with salad dressing on the side.

POTATO SALAD

6 c. cooked potatoes, diced (peel may be left on)
1 stalk celery, diced
1 c. grated carrot, or 1 c. sliced and steamed carrots
½ c. frozen peas, thawed
Option: ½ c. dill pickles, diced
1 bunch green onions, chopped
⅓ c. sliced radishes
Tofu Mayonnaise *see recipe pg. 39
Sea salt if needed

1. Mix all ingredients together. (Careful not to mash potatoes).
2. Spoon in enough tofu mayonnaise or commercial Nasoya Nayonaise to desired amount (approximately 1½ cup).
3. Place in a serving bowl. Smooth surface of salad and sprinkle with paprika.

MARINATED VEGETABLE MEDLEY

2 medium large carrots, sliced
1 small red onion diced in ½-inch cubes
1 red pepper diced in ½ - 1-inch cubes
1 green pepper diced in ½ - 1-inch cubes
3 c. fresh broccoli

Dressing:
⅓ c. olive oil
2 - 3 Tbsp. pure lemon juice
1 tsp. oregano
½ tsp. spike seasoning
½ tsp. garlic powder

1. Toss vegetables together gently.
2. Using a fork, whisk-dressing ingredients together.
3. Pour dressing over vegetables and let marinate in fridge for 2 - 3 hours before serving.

RICE SALAD

2 c. brown rice
4 c. water
½ tsp. sea salt
1 small onion, chopped fine
3 green onions, chopped
1 c. sliced black olives
1 c. chopped red and green peppers
¼ c. fresh parsley, chopped fine
2 c. cooked chickpeas
2 c. MGM Golden Nuggets diced into ½-inch pieces
1 c. grated carrot
½ c. olive oil
2 Tbsp. lemon juice

1. Bake rice in water in a covered casserole dish at 350 degrees F. for approximately 1 hour or until done. Mix in sea salt. Place rice in salad bowl and let cool.
2. Add vegetables, chickpeas, golden nuggets and olives.
3. Mix together lemon juice and oil. Pour over salad and mix well.
4. Chill in refrigerator.

FLAXSEED SALAD DRESSING

4 Tbsp. flax oil
2 tsp. onion powder
2 Tbsp. lemon juice
½ tsp. sea salt
4 Tbsp. water

1. Place all ingredients into a glass cup or bowl.
2. Whisk with a fork until well blended.
3. Serve over a tossed salad.

THOUSAND ISLAND SALAD DRESSING

¼ c. raw cashews
¼ c. water
2 Tbsp. lemon juice
½ lb. medium/firm tofu
½ tsp. sea salt
½ tsp. onion powder
1 tsp. honey
½ c. tomato sauce
¼ tsp. garlic powder
1 Tbsp. finely chopped dill pickles
1 Tbsp. finely chopped green and red peppers

1. Blend together all ingredients except pickles and peppers in a food processor until smooth.
2. Stir in pickles and peppers.
3. Marinate in fridge atleast 1 hour before serving.

A good replacement for vinegar is pure lemon juice. Vinegar irritates the stomach and makes the blood impure.

"The salads are prepared with oil and vinegar, fermentation takes place in the stomach, and the food does not digest, but decays or putrefies; as a consequence, the blood is not nourished, but becomes filled with impurities, and liver and kidney difficulties appear."
Counsels on Diet and Foods; E.G. White

Soups

BEANS

Prepare beans by first letting them soak overnight. Then drain and rinse them in cold water. Place the rinsed beans in a pot with just enough cold water to cover them. Cover the pot, bring them to a boil and drain again. Again pour in enough cold water to cover beans. Cover the pot, and again, bring to a boil. Then reduce the heat and let simmer until cooked. Once the beans are cooked they can be used immediately or frozen in small packages ready for your favorite recipes.

Approximate cooking times for different types of beans:

Bean Type	Cooking Time
• Garbanzoes	4 to 6 hours
• Green split peas	5 to 60 minutes
• Kidney beans	2 to 3 hours
• Lentils	45 to 60 minutes
• Navy beans	2 to 3 hours
• Pinto beans	2 to 3 hours
• Soy beans	4 to 6 hours
• Black beans	1½ to 2 hours
• Black-eyed peas	1 hour
• Great northern beans	2 hours
• Lima beans	1½ hours

GRAINS

Basically, all grains are cooked in the same manner. The difference is in the cooking time and the amount of water required. Place your measured grain in boiling water and add salt. Cover the pot and reduce the heat to simmer.

The following indicates the approximate cooking times for the different grains:

Grain	Amount	Water	Cooking Time
• Quick oats	1 cup	2 cups	5 minutes
• Large flake oats	1 cup	2 cups	30 minutes
• Whole oats	3/4 cup	2 cups	1 to 2 hours
• Pearl barley	1 cup	2 cups	45 minutes
• Oat bran	2/3 cup	2 cups	5 minutes
• Brown rice	1 cup	2 cups	1 hour
• Millet	1 cup	3 cups	1 hour
• Seven grain	1 cup	3 cups	1 hour
• Cornmeal	1 cup	4 cups	30 minutes

CREAM OF SPINACH SOUP

2 Tbsp. olive oil
2 medium onions, chopped
6 Tbsp. unbleached or whole-wheat pastry flour
1 tsp. sea salt
6 Tbsp. chicken-like seasoning
6 c. water
2 bunches fresh spinach, chopped
½ c. raw cashews
1 c. water

1. In a large pot, sautè onions in olive oil until onions turn clear in color.
2. Mix in flour, salt, chicken-like seasoning and 6 cups of water.
3. Stir and cook over medium heat until it boils and thickens.
4. Lightly steam spinach in a very small amount of water in medium pot on stove.
5. Blend in blender until smooth, cashews in 1 cup of water.
6. Add ½ of the steamed spinach to the blender and blend 2 seconds.
7. Mix remaining ½ of spinach to the large stockpot then stir in mixture from blender.
8. Heat until hot but do not boil.

5 BEAN SOUP

2 c. dried beans (5 kind mix)
12 c. water
1 large onion, chopped
1 c. celery, chopped ½ inch pieces
1 c. carrots, sliced
1 (14 oz) can diced tomatoes
2 c. potatoes, peeled and diced
1 tsp. sea salt
1 Tbsp. parley flakes
½ tsp. garlic powder
¼ tsp. thyme

1. Put beans and water in large pot.
2. Bring to a boil. Cover and simmer.
3. Add remaining ingredients.
4. Return to stove. Cover and simmer about 20 minutes until vegetables are tender.
5. Add more salt if needed.

CREAM OF CARROT SOUP

4 c. carrots, peeled and sliced
2 Tbsp. chicken-like seasoning
2 c. water
1 medium onion, chopped
3 Tbsp. unbleached white flour
½ tsp. sea salt
6 Tbsp. tofu or soy milk powder
6 c. water

1. Combine carrots, chicken-like seasoning, water and onion in saucepan. Cook until vegetables are tender. Do not drain.
2. Place in blender.
3. Add flour, salt and milk powder.
4. Blend until smooth.
5. Pour into large pot.
6. Add 6 cups of water.
7. Heat over medium heat. Constantly stir so it does not burn. Serve hot.

POTATO VEGETABLE SOUP

2 - 3 Tbsp. olive oil
1 large onion, diced
1 c. carrots, sliced
½ c. celery, chopped
1 garlic clove, minced
2 c. water
4 c. potatoes, peeled and diced
2 Tbsp. chicken-like seasoning
¾ tsp. sea salt
1 tsp. dry parsley flakes
2 c. tofu or soy milk

1. Put first 5 ingredients into large pot.
2. Sautè vegetables until onion is soft and clear.
3. Add water, potatoes, chicken-like seasoning, salt and parsley.
4. Bring to a boil. Cover and simmer slowly until vegetables are cooked. Stir occasionally.
5. Stir in soy/tofu milk. Heat without boiling.

CREAM OF ASPARAGUS SOUP

2 Tbsp. olive oil
1 small onion, chopped
2 Tbsp. unbleached white flour
½ tsp. sea salt
4 Tbsp. tofu or soy milk powder
3 c. water
1½ Tbsp. chicken-like seasoning
2 c. fresh asparagus, chopped

1. Sautè onion in oil until clear and soft.
2. Mix in flour, salt, milk powder, water and chicken-like seasoning.
3. Cook and stir over medium heat until it boils and thickens.
4. Steam asparagus in a little water. Add to soup.
5. Run soup through blender until smooth.
6. Add more salt if needed.

CREAM OF CAULIFLOWER SOUP #1

1 medium head of cauliflower
2 c. water
2 Tbsp. chicken-like seasoning
1 - 2 Tbsp. olive oil
1 medium onion, chopped
¼ c. unbleached white flour or whole-wheat pastry flour
¼ - ½ tsp. sea salt
2 c. soy milk

1. Cook cauliflower in water and chicken-like seasoning until tender. Do not drain.
2. Run through blender to desired texture. Set aside.
3. In large pot, sautè onion in oil until clear and soft.
4. Mix in flour, salt and soy milk.
5. Heat and stir until it boils and thickens.
6. Add cauliflower mixture. Heat to serve.

CREAM OF CAULIFLOWER SOUP #2

1 - 2 Tbsp. olive oil
1 medium onion, diced
6 c. water
1 tsp. sea salt
½ c. chicken-like seasoning
1 tsp. onion powder
½ tsp. granulated garlic powder
1 Tbsp. parsley flakes
2 stalks celery, chopped
2 carrots, diced
1 c. raw cashews
2 c. water
2 c. fresh cauliflower
1 c. frozen peas

1. In a large pot, sautè onion in oil until clear.
2. Stir in remaining ingredients except cashews, 2 cups of water, cauliflower and peas. Simmer until vegetables are tender.
3. Blend in blender until very smooth cashews and water. Add to soup along with cauliflower and peas. Simmer for 5 minutes then serve.

"BEEF" BARLEY SOUP

10 c. water
8 Tbsp. beef-like seasoning
1 small onion, chopped
2 carrots, diced
2 celery stalks, diced
1 c. pearl barley
1 c. TVP (soy beef chunks or granules)
¼ c. Bragg's liquid aminos
1 Tbsp. Spike seasoning, salt-free

1. Measure water into a large stockpot. Bring to a boil.
2. Add remaining ingredients.
3. Simmer about 20 - 30 minutes or until barley and vegetables are tender.

HEARTY MEDITERRANEAN SOUP

1 c. red lentils
2 Tbsp. olive oil
2 onions, chopped
1 - 2 garlic cloves, minced
¼ - ½ tsp. ginger powder
½ tsp. paprika
3 c. water
3 Tbsp. beef-like seasoning
1 - (28 oz) can diced tomatoes
1 - (19 oz) can chick peas, drained
Sea salt to taste
½ tsp. oregano
¼ - 1 tsp. crushed basil

1. In colander, rinse and drain lentils then set aside.
2. In large pot, sautè in oil, onion and garlic for 2 minutes.
3. Stir in ginger and paprika. Cook stirring for 1 minute.
4. Add lentils and stir well.
5. Stir in water, beef-like seasoning and tomatoes.
6. Bring to a boil over high heat. Reduce to medium low. Simmer covered 30-40 minutes or until lentils are done.
7. Stir in chickpeas, salt, oregano and basil.
8. Simmer uncovered 10 minutes. Serve.

SPLIT PEA SOUP

1 c. dry split peas
6 c. water
1 medium onion, diced
2 small stalks celery, diced
2 carrots, diced
2 Tbsp. chicken-like seasoning
¼ tsp. dried sweet basil
Sea salt to taste

1. Bring water to a boil in large pot.
2. Add split peas, onion, celery, carrots, and chicken- like seasoning.
3. Simmer until split peas and vegetables are tender.
4. Add basil and sea salt to taste.
5. Run through blender until smooth.
6. Reheat. Season with salt to taste. Serve with crackers.

CORN CHOWDER

6 c. water, or reserved "corn water" (from boiling corn on the cob)
4 medium potatoes, peeled
1 large onion, diced
1 large carrot, diced
4 large ears of corn boiled then corn stripped off or 3 c. frozen or canned whole kernel corn
½ tsp. garlic powder
1 tsp. sea salt or to taste
1 Tbsp. dry parsley
4 Tbsp. chicken-like seasoning
Options: cashew cream:
1 c. water blended with ½ c. raw cashews until smooth

1. In a large pot, bring corn water to a boil.
2. Cut 3 potatoes into 1-inch cubes and place in the pot.
3. Boil until potatoes are done. Scoop potatoes out of pot with a little broth and place in blender. Blend until smooth then place back in pot.
4. Dice up the last potato into small cubes and add to pot.
5. Stir in diced onion, carrots, and seasonings.
6. Simmer over low heat until vegetables are tender.
7. Add corn and cashew cream (if desired). Heat through, then serve.

TUSCAN BEAN SOUP

2 Tbsp. olive oil
1 large onion, sliced
2 - 3 garlic cloves, minced
2 medium carrots, thinly sliced
1 large rutabaga, peeled and sliced into strips (approx. ¼ inch. thick and 1-inch long)
4 c. shredded green cabbage
2 (16 oz) cans Lima beans, drained
1 (28 oz) can diced tomatoes with juice
6 c. water
6 Tbsp. beef-like seasoning
1 Tbsp. dry parsley flakes or 2 Tbsp. fresh chopped parsley
Sea salt to taste

1. Over medium heat, place oil in stockpot.
2. Sautè onion and garlic in oil until clear.
3. Add carrots and turnips. Cook for 2 minutes.
4. Stir in remaining ingredients and bring to a boil.
5. Cover and simmer until vegetables are tender (about 25 minutes).
6. Add sea salt to taste.

CREAM OF BROCCOLI SOUP

2 - 4 c. raw broccoli
1 - 2 c. water
¾ c. raw cashew pieces
1 Tbsp. nutritional yeast flakes
1 Tbsp. chicken-like seasoning
1 c. water
1½ Tbsp. lemon juice
4 tsp. onion powder
1 Tbsp. Bragg's liquid aminos
Sea salt for taste
4 c. water
3 Tbsp. cornstarch or 3 Tbsp. heaping arrowroot powder

1. Steam broccoli in 1 cup of water until tender.
2. Mash with potato masher.
3. Blend in blender until smooth, cashews, yeast flakes, chicken-like seasoning, 1 cup of water, lemon juice, onion powder, liquid aminos and cornstarch. Add to broccoli.
4. Pour in last 4 cups water.
5. Stir and add salt to taste.
6. Simmer until hot and soup appears slightly thickened.

**Variation: for a thicker soup, add some cooked mashed potatoes.

"CHICKEN NOODLE" SOUP

10 c. water
8 Tbsp. chicken-like seasoning
2 carrots, diced small
2 stalks celery, diced small
¾ tsp. salt
1 Tbsp. parsley flakes
250-300 g. linguini or spaghetti noodles
2 c. MGM frozen "Meatless Chicken Roll" diced.

1. In a stockpot, bring water to a boil.
2. Add vegetables and seasonings.
3. Break noodles into ⅛ pieces and add to pot.
4. Mix in meatless chicken and simmer until noodles and vegetables are tender.

BUTTERNUT SQUASH SOUP

1-2 Tbsp. oil
1 small onion, chopped
2 Tbsp. chicken-like seasoning
2 c. water
1 large potato, peeled and diced
½ tsp. sea salt
⅛ tsp. thyme
2 c. cooked and mashed squash
2 c. water
1 c. raw cashews

1. In a large pot sautè onion in oil or a little water until soft and clear.
2. Add chicken-like seasoning, 2 cups water, potato, salt and thyme. Cook over medium heat until potato is soft.
3. Place mixture in blender and blend until smooth. Return to pot.
4. Blend in blender until smooth, cashews in water.
5. Add cashew milk and squash to pot. Heat over low temperature stirring occasionally until desired temperature. Serve immediately.

CREAM OF ZUCCHINI SOUP #1

2 lbs. zucchini, unpeeled, sliced
1 medium onion, diced
1 garlic clove, minced
2 Tbsp. olive oil
2 c. water
4 Tbsp. chicken-like seasoning
1 tsp. lemon juice
½ tsp. sea salt or to taste
1 c. water
½ c. raw cashew pieces

1. Combine zucchini, onion, garlic and oil in pan. Sautè slowly while covered until soft, about 10 minutes.
2. Add 2 cups of water, chicken-like seasoning, lemon juice and salt.
3. Run through blender then return to pot. Heat.
4. Blend cashews in 1 cup of water until very smooth.
5. Add to zucchini mixture. Heat to serve.

CREAM OF ZUCCHINI SOUP #2

1½ lb. unpeeled zucchini, sliced
1/2 c. chopped onion
2 Tbsp. olive oil
2½ c. water
2½ Tbsp. chicken-like seasoning
½ tsp. basil
½ tsp. sea salt (optional)
1 c. water
1-3 c. raw cashew pieces

1. Sautè in olive oil zucchini and onion until tender in large pot.
2. Add 2½ cups of water, chicken-like seasoning, basil and sea salt.
3. Cook for 15 minutes over medium heat.
4. Run through blender then return to pot. Blend 1 cup of water and raw cashews in the blender until smooth.
5. Add to the large pot of soup. Heat through.
6. Do not bring to a boil (cashew cream may curdle). Serve and enjoy!

BORSCHT

10 c. water
3 Tbsp. beef-like seasoning
1 large onion, diced
2 garlic cloves, minced
3 medium beets, coarsely grated or diced small
2 carrots coarsely grated or diced small
1 c. diced celery
2 medium potatoes, diced
4 c. shredded cabbage
1 small can diced tomatoes or 3 fresh tomatoes diced
1 Tbsp. lemon juice
1 Tbsp. liquid aminos

1. Bring water to a boil.
2. Add seasoning, onion, garlic, beets and carrots. Simmer 15 minutes.
3. Add celery and potatoes. Cook for another 10 minutes.
4. Add cabbage, tomatoes, lemon juice and liquid aminos. Simmer until vegetables are tender.

• To make cream soup, blend in blender; cashews in water until smooth. Add cream to soup. Heat to serve.

MOM'S HOMEMADE VEGETABLE SOUP

2 Tbsp. olive oil
2 onions, chopped
1 (16 oz) can tomatoes, diced
1 c. beef-like gravy *see recipe pg. 41
3 potatoes, diced
½ c. elbow noodles
¼ c. pearl barley
¼ c. celery, chopped
1 can beans in tomato sauce
Sea salt to taste
8 - 10 c. water

1. Sautè onion in oil until soft.
2. Add remaining ingredients.
3. Place in glass casserole with lid and place in oven at 350 degrees F for about one hour or until done.
Suggestion: if using a pressure cooker, seal and cook 40 minutes.

TOMATO VEGETABLE SOUP

1 recipe of gluten broth *see recipe pg. 54
2 carrots, sliced
2 medium potatoes, diced
1 medium onion, diced
2 stalks celery
1 c. frozen peas or green beans

1. Bring gluten broth to a boil.
2. Place all ingredients into the pot of boiling broth. Simmer until vegetables are tender. Serve!

CREAM OF CELERY SOUP

3 c. water
3 c. celery, diced
½ tsp. garlic powder
1 tsp. onion powder
2 c. water
4 Tbsp. unbleached white flour
6 Tbsp. soy milk powder
2 Tbsp. chicken-like seasoning
1 tsp. sea salt

1. Bring 3 cups water to a boil in a large pot.
2. Add chopped celery, garlic powder and onion powder. Simmer until tender.
3. Blend in blender 2 cups water, flour, milk powder, chicken-like seasoning and salt.
4. Using a slotted spoon, scoop the cooked celery into the blender. Whiz gently in blender until celery is chopped. Pour celery mixture into hot broth in pot.
5. Simmer over medium heat until soup thickens.

LENTIL STEW

¾ c. celery, chopped
1 onion, chopped
1 c. carrots, sliced
2 c. potatoes, diced
1 c. dry lentils
1 tsp. sea salt
2 Tbsp. dry parsley
4 c. water
1 (28 oz) can diced tomatoes
¼ tsp. thyme
¼ tsp. garlic powder

1. Place all ingredients (except tomatoes) in pot.
2. Bring to a boil then simmer over low temperature for about ¾ hour.
3. Add tomatoes and cook for 10 more minutes.

VEGETABLE STEW

5 c. water
2 large potatoes, diced
4 carrots, diced
1 large onion, diced
2 large stalks celery, diced
1½ c. frozen peas
4 Tbsp. beef-like seasoning
1 tsp. sea salt
2 tsp. basil
1 c. water
½ c. unbleached white flour or whole-wheat flour
1 c. TVP (soy beef-like chunks)

1. Bring 5 cups of water to a boil. Add beef-like chunks.
2. Let simmer until chunks are soft (about 5 minutes).
3. Add carrots, potatoes, celery and onions. Cook until tender.
4. Whisk together flour and 1 cup water.
5. Add beef-like seasoning, basil and salt.
6. Pour into vegetable mixture slowly while stirring.
7. Simmer until stew thickens.
8. Add frozen peas. Simmer until heated through then serve with biscuits.

VEGETARIAN PASTA CHILI

1 - 2 Tbsp. olive oil
1 c. ground gluten or soaked TVP granules
1 large onion, chopped
2 (15 oz) can kidney beans (or 2 cups cooked)
1 (28 oz) can pureed tomatoes
1 (28 oz) can diced tomatoes
2 c. water
2 c. soy or brown rice, macaroni or spiral pasta
½ - 1 Tbsp. chili powder
Sea salt to taste

1. In large pot, sautè burger and onion in oil until lightly browned.
2. Add remaining ingredients and simmer until pasta is done.
3. Serve with cornbread. *see recipe pg. 29

**Variation: Black Bean Chili: replace the kidney beans with black beans.

HEARTY BEAN SOUP

1 Tbsp. olive oil
2 carrots, peeled and sliced
2 stalks celery sliced
1 onion, chopped
1 (19 oz) can or 2 c. cooked mixed beans
1 (28 oz) can diced tomatoes
3 Tbsp. beef-like seasoning
4 c. water
1 c. Rotini noodles
1 tsp. sea salt or to taste

1. Sauté in a large pot, carrots, celery and onion in olive oil or a little water for about 5 minutes.
2. Add remaining ingredients. Boil until vegetables and Rotini noodles are tender.
3. Serve immediately

Desserts

SUGAR FACTS

Did you know it takes 90 feet of sugar cane to make ½ cup white sugar?

Sugar is very refined and therefore taxes the liver and kidneys. One should try to avoid these refined sugars if possible. Too much refined sugar depletes the body of B vitamins. B vitamins are essential for healthy nerves. A depletion of B vitamins lowers our resistance to infection and makes us irritable and depressed.

Good substitutes would include granulated cane sugar, pure maple syrup, honey, rice syrup or barley syrup.

Sugar is:

1. A preservative and poison.
2. It alters metabolism causing excessive weight gain.
3. Restricts action of digestive enzymes; interferes with proper digestion of nutrients.
4. Develops a craving for alcohol.
5. Makes appetite control center go haywire.
6. Causes fermentation in the stomach
7. Breakdown of immune system.

Why Not Chocolate?

- Chocolate contains Methylxanthines a contributing factor to breast and prostate cancer.
- Tannin which has harmful effects on the mucous membranes of the digestive tract.
- Theobromine causes headaches, central nervous system irritation, itching, depression, anxiety, and fibrocystic disease of the breast.
- Sugar in large amounts is used to mask the bitter flavor and make it palatable.
- Fat, a minimum of 50%.
- Contamination: Cocoa beans come from countries with poor sanitation. The bean pods are left in piles outdoors to ferment for 3-8 days. Fermentation is essential to develop the chocolate flavor. Quantities of Aflatoxins, which are cancer promoting toxins produced by molds, are produced in the beans. In addition, insects, rodents, and small animals make nests in piles and many kinds of contamination occur. The U.S. Department of Health and Human Services lists contaminate levels in chocolate from "insects, rodents, and other natural contaminants" two ways:

1. Visible or solid animal excreta must not exceed 10 milligrams per pound.
2. Chocolate powder must not have more than 75 insect fragments in 3 tablespoons of powder.

- Many individuals thought to be allergic to chocolate may actually be allergic to the contaminants in the chocolate.

Carob powder contains no methylxanthines, no tannin, no theobromine, is naturally sweet, low in fat, and no fermentation necessary with no known allergy reactions.

BANANA NUT BREAD

1⅔ c. whole-wheat pastry flour
⅔ c. walnut or pecan pieces
½ tsp. sea salt
2 tsp. baking powder (alum. free)
1 tsp. finely grated orange or lemon peel
⅔ c. water
⅓ c. raw cashews
½ c. Sucanat or ⅓ c. honey
2 small ripe bananas
1 Tbsp. Ener-G egg replacer powder
1 tsp. lemon juice

1. Mix together dry ingredients and citrus peel in mixing bowl.
2. Place in blender, water, cashews, Sucanat or honey, bananas, egg replacer and lemon juice. Blend until very smooth. Pour into dry mixture and mix well.
3. Pour mixture into a greased bread pan.
4. Bake at 350 degrees F. for 1 hour or until toothpick comes out clean when tested.

CAROB PUDDING

2 c. water
⅔ c. raw cashews
1 tsp. vanilla
¼ tsp. sea salt
½ c. pure maple syrup
3 Tbsp. cornstarch
3 Tbsp. roasted carob powder
1 Tbsp. instant coffee substitute
⅓ c. carob chips (dairy-free and barley-malt sweetened)

1. Place all ingredients except carob chips in blender and blend until smooth.
2. Pour blended mixture into a small saucepan. Stir constantly over medium heat until sauce comes to a slow boil.
3. Remove pot from stove and stir in carob chips until chips are completely melted.
4. Pour into individual serving dishes.

• Excellent used as a pie or tart filling.

CAROB CAKE

2 c. unbleached white flour
¾ c. Sucanat
½ c. roasted carob powder
¼ tsp. sea salt
1 c. water
1 c. Nasoya Nayonnaise or Tofu Mayonnaise *see recipe pg. 39
2 tsp. vanilla extract
3 tsp. baking powder (alum. free)

1. Mix dry ingredients together. Sift out lumps.
2. Add remaining ingredients. Mix well.
3. Spread into a lightly greased 9x9-inch glass pan.
4. Bake at 350 degrees F. for approximately 30-40 minutes or until toothpick when tested comes out clean.

• This is a dark moist cake.

WHIPPED CREAM

1 can cold coconut milk
1 Tbsp. pure vanilla extract
1 Tbsp. liquid honey
2 Tbsp. Cleargel powder, (or as needed to thicken)

1. Place ingredients in blender. Blend until smooth and thickened.
2. Use immediately.

FRESH FRUIT PIE

1 Baked pie shell
2 c. Fresh fruit, sliced if desired
2 c. 100% pure fruit juice (use apple juice to obtain a clear glaze)
3 Tbsp. Cleargel powder, (or more if needed to thicken)
Honey to taste, if desired

1. Arrange fresh fruit in a pre-baked and cooled pie shell.
2. Pour juice and clear jel in blender. Blend until smooth and slightly thickened.
3. Add honey to taste if needed.
4. Pour over fruit and chill pie in fridge.
5. Serve with whipped cream. *see recipe pg. 113

CAROB LOGS

½ c. orange juice
3 Tbsp. minute tapioca
¼ c. liquid honey
1 c. ground almonds (reserve ½ c.)
1 c. ground walnuts or pecans
1 c. unsweetened fine shredded coconut
3 Tbsp. carob powder
1 c. finely chopped dates
1 Tbsp. vanilla

1. In a saucepan combine juice, tapioca and honey.
2. Cook over medium heat until tapioca softens and mixture slightly thickens.
3. Remove from heat. Stir in remaining ingredients except the ½ c. reserved almonds.
4. Shape into small logs and roll in reserved ground almonds. Chill.

NO BAKE CAROB COUSCOUS CAKE

¾ c. pecans, ground
2½ c. water
1 c. Sucanat — ½ cup
⅓ c. carob powder
⅓ c. pure maple syrup
1 Tbsp. instant coffee substitute
1 c. raw couscous
1 Tbsp. Pure vanilla extract

1. Roast ground pecans in 300 degrees F. oven for approximately 30 minutes or until brown. Remove from oven and let cool.
2. In saucepan, stir together water, Sucanat, carob powder, maple syrup, coffee substitute, and couscous. Bring to a simmer and cook until thickened 5 to 10 minutes.
3. Remove from heat. Add vanilla and stir well.
4. Spread mixture into a greased 9-inch springform pan.
5. Sprinkle ¼ c. ground pecan meal over the couscous cake.

Cream Topping:
1½ c. carob chips (sweetened with barley Malt and non-dairy)
2 (10 oz/300 g.) Pkg. Mori-Nu silken firm tofu (Room Temperature)
3 Tbsp. Pure maple syrup

1. Melt carob chips over low heat in small saucepan.
2. Transfer to blender; add tofu and maple syrup. Blend until smooth.
3. Pour over cake and top with remaining ground pecans.
4. Refrigerate until set, about 2 hours. Serve cold.

RASPBERRY TOFU CHEESECAKE

2 c. graham crumbs
⅓ c. oil
1 Tbsp. honey or Sucanat
1 can coconut milk
4 Tbsp. Clearjel powder
2 blocks Mori-Nu silken firm tofu
1 Pkg. lemon kosher-jel
1 Tbsp. honey
1 Tbsp. lemon juice
2 c. frozen raspberries
1 Tbsp. honey
1 Tbsp. cornstarch

1. Preheat oven to 400 degrees F.
2. Lightly grease a 9 or 12-inch springform pan.
3. Mix together graham crumbs, oil, and honey or Sucanat in a small bowl. Press into the bottom of the springform pan.
4. Bake in oven for 10 minutes or until golden brown. Let crust cool.
5. Blend coconut milk and Clearjel powder in blender until it has thickened. Pour into a bowl.
6. Place tofu, lemon jel, honey and lemon juice in blender. Blend until very smooth.
7. Mix tofu mixture together with thickened coconut milk. Pour on graham crust. Let it set up in fridge.
8. Place frozen fruit in saucepan. Allow fruit to melt. Stir in cornstarch and honey. Cook over medium heat until fruit becomes thickened and clear in color. Pour over tofu filling and chill in fridge a couple of hours or until set.

Serves 8-12 people

Variation: replace raspberries with the equivalent amount of strawberries, blueberries or other choice of fruit.

TAHINI CANDY

½ c. Tahini butter
1 tsp. pure vanilla extract
¼ c. pure maple syrup
⅓ c. carob powder
¼ c. unsweetened shredded coconut

1. Place tahini butter in a small bowl.
2. Mix in vanilla and maple syrup.
3. Press lumps out of carob powder using a sifter or fork.
4. Mix carob into the tahini paste using a fork until it is evenly mixed in.
5. Form into a log approximately 1-inch round. Roll in coconut including the ends.
6. Place on a plate or piece of wax paper.
7. Place in fridge or freezer to chill until firm. Once firm, cut into 1-inch pieces. Store in a container in the fridge or freezer. Always serve chilled.

APPLECAKE

6 - 8 medium/large apples
¼ tsp. sea salt
½ c. honey
1 tsp. vanilla
3 tsp. baking powder (alum. free)
⅓ c. safflower oil
1 c. soy or tofu milk
3 tsp. Ener-G egg replacer powder dissolved in 4 Tbsp. water
2 c. flour

1. Preheat oven to 375 degree F. Lightly grease a 9" x 12" glass baking dish.
2. Peel, core and slice apples into baking dish until apples fill the dish half full.
3. In a bowl, mix together remaining ingredients.
4. Place dough by spoonfuls evenly over apples with the back of the spoon, gently spread mixture. Strive to make it even and smooth.
5. Bake in oven for 25-30 minutes, or until golden brown.

DAD'S OATMEAL DATE CAKE

1 c. quick oats
1 c. dates, chopped
1½ c. boiling water
⅓ c safflower oil
¾ c. Sucanat or ½ c. honey
3 tsp. Ener-G egg replacer powder, dissolved in 4 Tbsp. of water
1 tsp. vanilla
1½ c. unbleached white flour
2 tsp. baking powder (alum. free)
1 tsp. cinnamon
½ tsp. sea salt

Topping: ¾ c. brown sugar
⅓ c. thick soy milk
¼ c. safflower or olive oil
1 c. coconut

1. Mix oats and dates together.
2. Pour boiling water over top of mixture. Let cool.
3. Add remainder of cake ingredients into oat mixture.
4. Pour into a lightly greased 9-inch springform pan.
5. Bake at 350 degrees F. for 35-40 minutes, or until cake is lightly browned (test by using a toothpick).

Topping:
6. In a small pot, mix together all topping ingredients.
7. Bring to a boil and boil for 1 minute.
8. Carefully spread on cake.
9. Broil in oven until golden brown.
10. Remove from oven and place pecan halves in an arranged pattern over the top.

CAROB CARAMELS

1 c. unsweetened coconut
½ c. carob powder
1 c. soy or tofu milk powder
½ c. liquid honey
1 tsp. vanilla
¼ tsp. sea salt
2 Tbsp. Better Than Butter *see recipe pg. 37
¼ c. almonds, finely ground

1. Combine all ingredients together, except almonds. (You may need to use your hand or a food processor).
2. Press firmly and smoothly into a 9 X 9-inch pan.
3. Sprinkle with almonds. Press down gently.
4. Chill 2 hours in fridge. Cut into squares and serve chilled. Store squares in fridge or freezer.

TROPICAL DELIGHT

1 graham crust
2 Tbsp. plain kosher gel or powdered agar agar
¾ c. pineapple juice
1 c. boiling water
⅓ c. honey
1 c. raw cashews
¼ c. unsweetened coconut
¼ tsp. sea salt
6 ice cubes
2 (10 oz) cans crushed pineapple
1 Tbsp. cornstarch
1Tbsp. honey

1. In blender, place kosher-jel plain or agar agar and pineapple juice (use from 1 can of crushed pineapple). Let stand for 10 minutes. Pour in boiling water. Blend briefly until gelatin is dissolved.
2. Add honey, cashews, coconut and salt. Blend until smooth and creamy.
3. Add ice cubes. Blend until smooth.
4. Pour mixture into bowl and stir in 1 can drained crushed pineapple. Pour over baked graham crust in a 10-inch spring form pan. Chill until set.
5. In a saucepan mix together, 1 can crushed pineapple including juice, cornstarch dissolved in water and honey, cook until mixture is thickened and turns clear. Pour over chilled dessert.
6. Return to fridge and again chill until set. Cut and serve.

EAT-MORE BARS

1 c. carob chips (barley-malt sweetened)
½ c. Rogers golden syrup or liquid honey (Rogers brand is pure cane, other
    brands are refined sugars)
½ c. peanut butter (smooth)
1 c. wheat germ
½ c. raw sunflower seeds
1 c. dry roasted peanuts, chopped

1. Melt together carob chips, syrup/honey and peanut butter in a non-stick
   saucepan. Remove from heat.
2. Stir in remaining ingredients. Press into a 9 X 9-inch pan.
3. Chill and then cut into squares. Serve chilled. (These freeze well).

BLUEBERRY PIE

1 grape nut pie crust, pg. 120
2 c. frozen blueberries
1 c. frozen grape juice concentrate, undiluted
¼ c. minute tapioca
1 tsp. pure vanilla extract
1 Tbsp. lemon juice

1. In medium pot place tapioca in grape juice. Let stand for 5 minutes.
   Bring to a boil; simmer while stirring for 5 minutes.
2. Stir in blueberries. Simmer 5 minutes or until tapioca granules are clear.
3. Pour into baked piecrust. Chill in fridge until firm.

GRAPE NUT PIE CRUST

1 c. chopped dates
⅓ c. water
¾ c. grape nuts
½ c. quick oats
¼ c. finely ground almonds
¼ tsp. sea salt

1. Bring water and dates to a boil. Simmer until dates are soft. Mash with
   potato masher.
2. Mix in remaining ingredients.
3. Press into a pie plate. Bake at 375 degrees F. for 10 minutes.
   Cool, then add filling.

CAROB BALLS

1 c. peanut butter unsweetened and smooth
1 c. chopped dates softened in microwave with a little water
⅓ c. honey
1 c. finely ground almonds
1 c. roasted wheat germ
1 c. tofu or soy milk powder
3 Tbsp. apple juice
2 c. carob chips (barley malt sweetened)

1. Mix together all ingredients except carob chips. (You will need to use your hands).
2. Melt carob chips in double boiler or in pot over low heat.
3. Form a ball out of first mixture. Dip in melted carob and place on cookie sheet. Repeat until mixture is used up. Chill in fridge. These freeze well and make nice gifts.

BANANA OATMEAL COOKIES

1 c. quick cooking oats
¾ c. unbleached white flour or whole wheat pastry flour
½ c. brown sugar or Sucanat
½ c. raisins
½ tsp. baking powder (alum free)
¼ c. oil or ½ c. vegan Canoleo margarine
1 Tbsp. Rogers pure golden cane syrup
½ c. mashed banana

1. In medium bowl, combine oats, flour, sugar, raisins and baking powder. Set aside.
2. In a small saucepan over medium heat mix together oil or margarine, syrup and banana. Bring to a simmer.
3. Stir banana mixture into oat mixture mixing well.
4. Drop by tablespoon full onto a lightly greased cookie sheet. Bake 10-15 minutes until golden brown.

• Makes about 18 cookies.

CARROT PIE

1 c. dates
2½ Tbsp. cornstarch
½ tsp. sea salt
3 Tbsp. unbleached white flour
1 tsp. pure vanilla
3 Tbsp. oil
2 c. cooked carrots
1½ c. soy or tofu milk
1 tsp. cinnamon
¼ tsp. ground cloves
¼ tsp. allspice
1 Basic pie crust *see recipe pg. 123

1. Place all ingredients into a blender. Blend until very smooth.
2. Pour into an unbaked pie shell.
3. Bake at 350 degrees F. for 35 minutes or until filling appears set.
Variation: pumpkin or a variety of squash can be substituted for the carrots.

PUMPKIN PIE FILLING

1 pkg. Mori-Nu silken firm tofu
1 (14 oz) can pumpkin
½ c. Sucanat
1 tsp. vanilla
½ tsp. sea salt
1½ tsp. cinnamon
¼ tsp. nutmeg
¼ tsp. allspice
¼ c. oil

1. Preheat oven to 350 degrees F.
2. Place all ingredients into blender. Blend until very smooth.
3. Pour into unbaked pie shell. Bake in oven for 1 hour or until filling
   appears set.

BASIC PIE CRUST

2 c. whole wheat pastry flour
¾ tsp. sea salt
2 Tbsp. wheat germ
½ c. boiling water
½ c. oil

1. Combine dry ingredients and make a well in the center.
2. Pour into the well the oil then water. Stir vigorously with a fork, slowly blending into dry ingredients.
3. Form a ball using your hands.
4. Roll out between wax paper to make a double piecrust or press into 2 - 10 inch pie plates using your hands.
5. Poke holes using a fork along bottom of crust if prebaking.
6. Bake at 350 degrees F. until golden brown.

CAROB CRISPS

½ c. liquid honey
1 c. crunchy pure peanut butter
1 c. carob chips (barley-malt sweetened and dairy-free)
3 c. Crisp or Puffed Rice Cereal

1. Melt in a large saucepan honey and peanut butter.
2. Remove from heat. Stir in carob chips until melted.
3. Mix in rice cereal.
4. Press into a 9 X 9-inch pan. Chill. Cut into squares and serve.

CAROB CHIP PECAN CAKE

2 c. raw cashews pieces
⅔ c. liquid honey
4 tsp. Ener-G egg replacer powder
2 tsp. vanilla
½ tsp. sea salt
2 c. cold water
4 tsp. baking powder (alum. free)
2 c. unbleached white flour
¾ c. pecan pieces
¾ c. carob chips (no sugar, no dairy, and no hydrogenated oil)

1. Blend in blender first six ingredients until smooth.
2. Pour blended mixture into a large bowl.
3. Add remaining ingredients. Mix well.
4. Pour into a lightly greased 9 X 12-inch glass cake pan. Bake at 350 degrees F. for 30 minutes or until lightly browned.

Icing: ¾ c. carob chips
    1 (10 oz or 300 g.) pkg. Mori-Nu silken tofu firm
    3 Tbsp. pure maple syrup

5. Melt carob chips in saucepan over low heat.
6. Transfer to blender and add tofu and maple syrup.
7. Blend until smooth. Pour over cooled cake. Refrigerate until set.

APPLE CRISP

6 medium apples
½ c. raisins
1 Tbsp. cinnamon
¼ c. oil (you may need to add more if using brown sugar)
1 c. quick oats
¼ c. pure maple syrup or ½ c. brown sugar
½ c. whole-wheat pastry flour

1. Peel and core apples. Slice apples ¼ inch thick into a 9 X 9-inch pan.
2. Sprinkle raisins and cinnamon over apples.
3. Mix together oil, oats, maple syrup and flour. Crumble over top of apples.
4. Place in a preheated 350 degrees F. oven. Bake for 40 minutes or until golden brown.

CAROB ZUCCHINI CAKE

2½ c. unbleached white flour
½ c. carob powder
4 tsp. baking powder (alum free)
½ tsp. sea salt
1 tsp. cinnamon
½ c. oil
1 c. honey
6 tsp. Ener-G egg replacer powder dissolved in 8 Tbsp. water
2 tsp. pure vanilla extract
2 c. grated zucchini, peeled
½ c. soy milk
½ c. unsweetened applesauce
Option: ½ c. chopped nuts
Powdered icing sugar

1. Preheat oven to 350 degrees F.
2. Mix together first 5 ingredients. Crush lumps of carob with fork if needed. Make a well in the center. Measure in remaining ingredients (except icing sugar). Mix thoroughly.
3. Pour into a greased 10-inch tube pan. Spread around evenly. Bake 45 min. - 1 hour or until done when tested with a toothpick. Let cake cool on wire cake rack.
4. Lightly sprinkle top of cake with icing sugar.

CAROB ZUCCHINI BANANA CAKE

2½ c. whole-wheat pastry flour
¾ c. carob powder
4 tsp. baking powder (alum free)
½ tsp. sea salt
1 tsp. cinnamon
½ c. oil
1 banana, mashed
1½ c. Sucanat
6 tsp. Ener-G egg replacer powder dissolved in 8 Tbsp. water
1 tsp. vanilla
2 c. grated zucchini, peeled
¾ c. soy milk

1. Preheat oven to 350 degrees F.
2. Mix together first 5 ingredients. Crush all lumps out with a fork. Make a well in the center. Measure in remaining ingredients. Mix well.
3. Pour into a greased 9 X 9-inch glass cake pan. Bake 1 hour or until toothpick when pricked comes out clean.

STRAWBERRY DREAM DESSERT

2 c. graham crumbs
¼ c. canoleo margarine melted or olive oil
¼ c. honey or Sucanat

Mix together crumb mixture. Press into a 9 X 12-inch pan. Bake at 375 degrees F. until golden brown. Let cool.

In a medium saucepan, melt together:
½ c. soymilk
1 Pkg. kosher marshmallows.
Remove from heat and chill slightly.

Blend in blender until thick:
1 can coconut milk
3 - 4 Tbsp. Clearjel powder
1 Tbsp. honey or Sucanat
1 Tbsp. vanilla

Add to marshmallow mixture and mix well. Spread over crumb crust. Chill in fridge.

In a separate bowl mix together:
2 c. frozen strawberries, sliced and thawed
8 Tbsp. strawberry kosher jel
1 c. boiling water

Pour over marshmallow layer. Chill in fridge. Slice into squares and serve. Serves approximately 12 people.

GINGERBREAD COOKIES

⅓ c. oil
⅓ c. honey or ½ c. Sucanat
½ c. molasses
⅓ c. water
3 c. whole-wheat pastry flour
1 tsp. baking powder (alum. free)
1 tsp. ginger powder
½ tsp. cinnamon
¼ tsp. ground cloves
¼ tsp. sea salt

1. In a large mixing bowl, mix ingredients together well.
2. Roll dough out on a lightly floured board.
3. Cut dough into shapes of gingerbread men.
4. Bake in preheated oven at 350 degrees F. for 8-10 minutes or until golden brown.

CARROT CAKE

¼ c. oil
¾ c. unsweetened applesauce
½ c. honey
½ c. raisins
Option: ½ c. chopped pecans or walnuts
2 c. grated carrot
1½ tsp. cinnamon
¼ tsp. nutmeg
½ c. soymilk
2 c. flour
3 tsp. baking powder (alum. free)
½ tsp. sea salt
4½ tsp. Ener-G egg replacer powder dissolved in 6 Tbsp. water

1. Combine all ingredients. Mix well.
2. Spread into a 9 X 13-inch greased pan.
3. Bake at 350 degrees F. for 50 minutes or until done when tested with a toothpick.

CAROB CHIP OATMEAL COOKIES

1½ c. whole-wheat pastry flour
⅔ c. chopped pecans
½ tsp. sea salt
2 c. rolled oats
1 c. carob chips (non-dairy and barley-malt sweetened)
½ c. oil
1 Tbsp. vanilla
½ c. honey
1 Tbsp. lemon juice
½ c. hot water

1. Mix together dry ingredients.
2. Stir in remaining ingredients and mix in well.
3. Let sit 10 minutes to allow dry ingredients to moisten.
4. Drop by tablespoon on a lightly greased cookie sheet.
5. Bake in oven at 350 degrees F. for about 20-25 minutes or until golden brown.

BANANA-STRAWBERRY SHERBET

3 frozen bananas
6 frozen strawberries

1. Place frozen fruit in food processor.
2. Blend until smooth. (Careful to not let it run too long or it will begin to melt.)
3. Serve immediately.

My Kitchen Prayer

Lord, bless these hands
  as they prepare
the daily meals
  with loving care.
May this kitchen by a place
  where those who eat
receive your grace.

Special Treats & Party Foods

BANANA SHAKE

2 whole frozen bananas
8 Tbsp. soy or tofu milk powder
2 Tbsp. vanilla extract
2½ c. cold water
12 ice cubes

1. Place all ingredients into blender
2. Blend until very smooth. Serve immediately.

RASPBERRY PUNCH

1 Frozen can unsweetened raspberry concentrate
1 Frozen can lemonade
2 Liters carbonated spring water
1 Liter cold purified water

Mix ingredients together.
Serve with slices of fresh lemon for garnish.

HOT FRUIT CIDER

2 L. unsweetened apple juice
1 L. unsweetened orange juice
1 L. fruit sweetened cranberry juice (Knudsen)
4 cinnamon sticks
8-10 whole cloves
1 mandarin orange divided into sections

Place all ingredients in large pot or crock-pot. Heat over medium
temperature and simmer for atleast 30 minutes before serving.

NACHOS

1 recipe "cheese sauce" *see recipe pg. 41
Option: jalapeno peppers, minced
1 Pkg. baked corn chips
3 - 4 medium tomatoes, diced
1 bunch green onion, chopped
1 can sliced black olives

1. Add minced jalapeno peppers to taste to 1 recipe of fresh made "cheese sauce".
2. Place each ingredient in separate bowls to self-serve at a party.
3. Layer corn chips, pour cheese-sauce over chips, sprinkle with diced tomatoes, green onion, and olives. Eat with fingers and enjoy!

POPCORN

½ c. popcorn kernels
⅓ c. flaxseed or olive oil
1 Tbsp. nutritional yeast flakes
Option: ½ tsp. garlic powder
Option: 1 tsp. spike seasoning

1. Pop popcorn in hot air popper.
2. Mix oil and seasonings together.
3. Pour evenly over popcorn and mix well. Serve warm.

SPINACH DIP

1½ c. Nasoya Nayonaise salad dressing or tofu mayonnaise *see recipe pg. 39
2 c. tofu sour cream *see recipe pg. 39
1 Pkg. Knorr vegetable dehydrated soup mix
1 (8 oz) can chopped water chestnuts, drained
3 green onions, chopped
1 (10 oz) Pkg. frozen chopped spinach, thawed and drained

1. Mix together well. Refrigerate 2 hours before serving.
2. Serve in hollowed out round or oval multigrain bread *see recipe pg. 24
3. Place pieces of bread pulled out of center, with raw vegetables around the loaf for dipping.

Sectional Index

Alphabetical Index

TASTE SENSATIONS

from ◄◄◄ MGM BRANDS ►►►

All Natural and Completely Meatless

A fabulous line up of vegetarian entrées and meal makers. Every item is all natural, highly nutritious and temptingly tasty. Our meaty and hearty foods are sure to satisfy the whole family.

 **Tofu Franks:** A delicious hot dog wiener with the goodness of tofu. All natural ingredients, completely vegetarian and good nutritional value. Great for the whole family, for BBQs or for quick lunches. Regular and jumbo sizes. Fresh or Frozen.

Meatless Breakfast Links: Hearty and juicy breakfast sausage with a zesty flavour and sizzling good taste. Easy and quick to prepare, on a skillet or in a microwave. Contains no artificial ingredients, no saturated fats or meat products.

 **Sam-Burger, Golden Burger:** Two great burger tastes for the BBQ grill. A choice, juicy beef flavoured burger or a light tasting, tender chik'n flavoured patty. For meaty sauces or dishes, chop up the patties and mix into spaghetti sauce, lasagna, chili or tacos.

Golden Nuggets: Succulent chik'n like pieces, in a golden, light, crispy batter. Just heat in the oven and serve with dipping sauce. Other serving ideas include Sweet and Sour Chik'n, BBQ shish-ka-bobs and sliced into Stir Fry chik'n and vegetables.

 **Deli Cuts: Bologna, Salami, Corned Beef, Chik'n, and Turkey** – flavoured cold cuts. Choose from our great line up for fabulous vegetarian sandwiches and salads. Nutritious and delicious for lunches and snacks for the whole family.

Notes

		Sunday	Monday	Tuesday
Week #1	Breakfast	**Apple Tortillas** Hot Drink	**Granola** Toast **Strawberry Jam** Fresh Banana & Pear	**Whole Wheat Pancakes** Peanut Butter Applesauce Fresh Blueberries
	Lunch	**Sweet 'n Sour Tofu** **Baked Brown Rice** **Bok Choy Salad** Corn **Banana Oatmeal Cookies**	**Lentil Roast** Baked Potatoes Steamed Broccoli **Cheese Sauce** Vegetable Platter **Carob Zucchini Cake**	**Macaroni Casserole** **Marinated Vegetable Medley** Fresh Sliced Tomatoes & Cucumbers **Dad's Oatmeal Cake**
	Supper	**Banana Strawberry Sherbet** Bran Muffins	**Black Bean Salad** **Thousand Island Salad Dressing**	**Pocket Bread** **Sliceable Cheese** Shredded Lettuce, Diced Tomatoes, Sliced Olives, Bean Sprouts **Tofu Mayonnaise**
		Sunday	Monday	Tuesday
Week #2	Breakfast	**Cashew-Oat Waffles** **Pear Cream** Fresh Strawberries	**Banana Nut Bread** Multigrain Porridge Fresh Apples & Grapes	**Scrambled Tofu** **Herbed Potatoes** Ketchup Toast with Olive Oil Brushed on Lightly Tomato Wedges
	Lunch	**Tofu Millet Burgers** **Ketchup, Mayo, Buns** Salad Plate Baked Fries Coleslaw **Tropical Delight**	**Alfredo Sauce** Fettuccini Noodles **Stir Fry Vegetables**	**Vegetable Stew** **Western Biscuits** **Better than Butter** Raw Vegetable Platter
	Supper	**Cream of Celery Soup** **Oat Crackers with Humus**	**Homemade Pizza** Raw Veggies **Tofu Mayonnaise (as a dip)**	**Applecake** **Pear Cream** Hot Drink

Wednesday	Thursday	Friday	Saturday
Apples 'n Rice Fresh Orange Slices	**Oatmeal** Grapefruit Toasted Bagel **Apricot Jam** **Mock Cream** **Cheese**	**Breakfast Tofu** **Drink** Fresh Fruit Salad Raw Nuts & Seeds	**French Toast** Pure Maple Syrup Cantelope Melon
Vegetable Tofu **Crepes** **Fried Rice** **Salad Platter** **Carob Crisps**	**Tasty Black** **Bean Burgers** Ketchup, Mayo, Buns, Lettuce, Tomato, Carrot & Celery Sticks **Potato Salad** **Carrot Pie with** **Whipped Cream**	**Shepherd's Pie** Corn on Cob Caesar Salad **Carob Pudding**	**Nutloaf** Mashed Potatoes **Beef Gravy** Tossed Salad **Flaxseed Dressing** **Baked Carrots** **Raspberry Tofu** **Cheesecake**
Cream of **Cauliflower** Soup #2 **Potato Dough** **Buns** **Better Than Butter**	**Rice Salad** Toast with Olive Oil & Garlic Powder	**Vegetarian** **Pasta Chili** **Cornbread**	**Nachos and** **Cheese Sauce**

Wednesday	Thursday	Friday	Saturday
Tropical **Surprise** **Muffins** Fresh Kiwi & Mango Dry Cereal Nutmilk or Soymilk	**Tofu Crepes** Strawberry Topping Whipped Cream	**Sweet Rolls** Fresh Fruit Platter	**Apple Crisp** Pear Cream Banana
Rice Stacks Guacamole **Tofu Sour Cream** **Carob Pudding**	**Vegetarian Fish** **Sticks** **Tartar Sauce** **Greek Salad** Scalloped Potatoes Steamed Brocolli & **Cheese Sauce** **Eatmore Bars**	**Vegetarian** **Lasagna** Cooked Peas **Multigrain Bread** **Better Than Butter** **with Garlic** Salad & Dressing **Tahini Candy**	**Turkey &** **Dressing** **Chicken Gravy** **Stuffed Baked** **Potatoes** Steamed Asparagus Tossed Salad **Carrot Cake**
Split Pea Soup Toast	**Veggie Fajitas** **Tofu Sour Cream**	**Pitachips** Hearty Mediterranean Soup	**Banana Shake** Popcorn

Notes

Notes

Notes

Great Gift Idea!

Give a "Vegetarian For Life" cookbook to a friend!

Order From: Darlene Blaney
C/o Nature's Promise Health Foods
2834 Morley Trail N.W.
Calgary, AB. Canada
T2M 4G7
(403)-220-0606

Send to:

Name: _____

Address: _____

_____

City: _____

Province or State: _____

Postal Code / Zip: _____ Phone Number: _____

Please send _____ copies of "Vegetarian For Life" to above address.

The cost is $17.95 plus GST per book plus $5.00 shipping and handling payable in Canadian funds.

Total enclosed:_____

Please make cheque or money order payable to: Darlene Blaney

Price subject to change without notice.
email: blaneyd@cadvision.com   http://members.home.net/vegetarianforlife